BOULANGERIE

The Craft and Culture of Baking in France

PAUL RAMBALI

With recipes and photographs by Maria Rudman

MACMILLAN • USA

MACMILLAN
A Prentice Hall Macmillan Company
15 Columbus Circle
New York, NY 10023

Library of Congress Cataloging-in-Publication Data
Rambali, Paul.
    Boulangerie / Paul Rambali; with recipes and photographs by Maria Rudman.
    p. cm.
    Includes index.
    ISBN 0-02-600865-3
    1. Bread. 2. Bakers and bakeries—France—History. I. Title.
TX769.R29 1995
641.8'15—dc20   94-5372 CIP

Manufactured in the United States of America

10 9 8 7 6 5 4 3 2 1

First Edition

BOULANGERIE

To Mikaela and Gustave for being patient and eating all the cakes.

ACKNOWLEDGMENTS

Thanks to Maria, for teaching Paul to bake; Margareta Rudman, for teaching her; Sven Rudman, for his camera; our agent, Carla Glasser, for making it possible; Morton and Barbara Kligerman and their daughter, Valli; Agnes Bonnet; Randall Koral; Ruth Marshall for reading the manuscript; our painstaking editor, Pam Hoenig; Evie Righter, for testing the recipes; Daniel Bertaux; Monsieur Sender for his library; Alain and Joelle Michaud; Gisela Wunderwald; Cornelia Von Einem; all the *boulangers* and *pâtissiers* who have been so generous with their time and skills, especially Roland Amon, Bernard Boisguerin, Basil Kamir, Jean-Luc Poujauran, Jean Jeudon, and Claude Moreau.

INTRODUCTION

This book began as I watched the demolition of an old *boulangerie*. Disheartened to see nothing left of the hundred-year-old premises, I shuffled along to another bakery, just down the street, to buy my baguette. It wasn't evident at first, but more had been lost in the rubble than the painted-glass signs and wrought-iron fittings. As we stood in line, I heard my neighbors exchange whispers. "It's a shame," they murmured. "The bread just isn't the same." The baguettes were long and golden, but something was lacking. I noticed that a hollowness had crept into the exchange of pleasantries between the staff and customers.

A few months later, the old bakery reopened. The murals on the ceiling—brown from decades of baking butter-rich croissants—were gone. Instead of celestial rays from painted cherubs, light from halogen lamps shone down on the loaves. The *pâtisseries*, which before used to grow tired as the day wore on, looked permanently fresh in new refrigerated displays. The same polite, hurrying shopgirls stood behind the counter. Instead of simply handing it over, they gave me my baguette in a long paper bag with a brand name on it.

From them I learned that the old baker had retired, and the *boulangerie* had been taken over by the owner of the bakery down the street. We never saw him emerge in a cloud of flour from the back, ruddy-faced from the heat of the oven, like the old baker. He was upstairs in an office. One morning, I saw a tanker delivering something down a long tube into the basement. It was dough for the branded baguettes, prerisen and semirefrigerated by the mill that had also financed the takeover. In the line, the grumbles continued.

At the same time, my wife, Maria, had begun making a photographic record of old, fast-disappearing *boulangeries*. As we talked to bakers, we heard complaints that seemed typical of beleaguered craftsmen, but we sensed a deeper loss. Despite immense and justified pride in their art, none wanted their children to become bakers—unless it was to achieve the prestige and financial rewards of the *pâtissier*.

If a cobbler goes out of business because of competition from mass-produced shoes, it doesn't stir the same anxieties as the closure of a bakery. At once banal and profound, bread is at the heart of French society. More than just a source of nourishment, bread is a fundamental token of community. The word *companion*, for instance, comes from the French word for bread, *pain*. A com*pan*ion is someone with whom you share your *pain*. The landscape around Paris, where we live, belongs to bread: wide plains of wheat slowly ripening to a deep sun-kissed yellow; towns identified by their church spires and grain silos. Bread allowed France to thrive; its scarcity brought famine and, finally, revolution.

The world envies the French their daily bread, a gastronomic delight the French have until lately taken for granted. The typical French family buys bread three times a day, for without it there would be no freshly buttered *tartines* at breakfast, nowhere to spread *pâté*, no means to soak up the bourguignon gravy, and nothing to eat with cheese and wine. Flecks of stiff brown crust on a white tablecloth are for me the sign of a satisfying meal. And a good baguette will make up for all manner of culinary disappointment.

In the line at the local *boulangerie*, the grumbles eventually ceased. We could still go elsewhere for good, artisan-made bread. But the brand-name baguettes were really quite satisfactory and I think we began to forget the difference. The baking profession rightly worries that the French eat less bread than before. The reason is not, as they suppose, that affluence has made us reject humble bread, but that traditions which elsewhere in Europe and North America have all but vanished are dying out in France.

It was to capture some of these vanishing—but also evolving—traditions that we have tried to bring together here everything you would find in a *boulangerie.* We talked with some master bread-makers and exponents of the evanescent art of *pâtisserie,* and we went in search of the country-style bread that's enjoying a nostalgic revival, to find out what makes French baking so special.

I

Surrounded by wheat fields, Paris thrives on bread. There, the craft of baking flourishes.

A green cleaning truck marked *Ville de Paris* passes by, sluicing down the streets with water, as Guyot arrives at the *boulangerie.* The truck goes by every morning at the same time. Apart from a few late-night revelers returning home, the Avenue Victor Hugo is quiet.

Guyot takes a last look along the sidewalk, at the row of grand apartment blocks whose occupants slumber behind closed metal shutters. He sniffs the air and takes note of the clear, starry sky. It means the bread will rise easily. He doesn't envy the city its sleep. The nocturnal peace gives him the tranquil space in which to do his job. By the morning, all these people will be awake and hungry, demanding their daily bread.

He unlocks the side door and descends the steep stone steps to the cellar. They are uneven—great hunks of stone buffed smooth and rubbed concave with wear. Though it is dark, Guyot knows his way. He has been the *maître* at this *boulangerie* for more than ten years. On the way down he can hear the hum of the refrigerators. The dough inside, prepared the previous day and placed in baskets lined with jute cloth, has been rising slowly. Switching on the lights, he hears the buzz of neon, a sound that has always accompanied his thoughts as he works. Today is Sunday, and already he is preparing mentally for this busiest day of the week.

The cellar is a long, vaulted tunnel; at the far end is a stainless steel oven more than six feet tall. The roof of the cellar is high, allowing air to circulate—unlike the cellars of some bakeries where Guyot has worked. The cellar had been dug out to accommodate the huge, deep oven with five narrow floors, each with a separate horizontal door. Lifting one, Guyot eyes the glow of the brick walls inside. The oven is still warm, like an eternal hearth, a flicker of life in the cold night. There is a woosh of gas as he relights it.

In front of the oven is a long rack equipped with a canvas stretcher on rollers, a contraption designed to load and unload dozens of baguettes at a time. The worn stone floor and tidy arrangement of tools suggest busy organization. Lengths of jute cloths lie folded in concertinas on a wooden rack, waiting to carry rows of baguettes. Flat wooden spades with long handles are propped to one side of the doors; more spades jut out from a rack above the oven. The rest of the narrow space in the cellar is taken up by refrigerators and kneading machines that look like giant blenders, with blades as big as propellers poised over deep metal tubs. Their large electric motors are doused in white dust. In fact, the dust is everywhere—fine white flour that lies in a film, softening contours and colors, penetrating pores and cracks.

The walls of the cellar are bare, gray stone. At the base of the outside walls, set back at intervals, are a number of grilles which appear from the outside to be about a foot high from the sidewalk. Now covered with wire mesh, they had been jammed open at one point and painted over since, sometime in the 1950s. The grilles allow the hot smells that rise from the *fournil,* the baking room, to escape at strategic points— just under the window filled with *pâtisseries* and near the main door. It's an irresistible smell, slightly sour and slightly sweet, fulsome and appetizing. Often thought of as a yeasty odor, it's the simple, primordial smell of the roasting milled wheat itself.

The grilles also serve to let some light and air into the basement kitchen, reminding the bakers that there is a time frame other than that of the bread, as well as keeping them aware of any changes in pressure or humidity that might affect the dough. The contact with the outside is welcome, but it's considered bad luck for bakers to go upstairs. Doused in flour from their shoes to their eyebrows, often shirtless and half roasted, themselves, from the heat of the oven, as well as bleary-eyed from lack of sleep, they are said to frighten the customers. Through the grilles, they can still keep an eye on comings and goings.

As an apprentice, one of the first things Guyot learned from the *mitron,* the baker's boy, was that from certain vantage points in the cellar *fournils* one could peek through the grilles at women who were pausing to admire the cakes on display in the window upstairs. This lesson was immediately followed by a slap to the back of the head by the master baker, who took Guyot's place to see what the fuss was about. He at once recognized the petticoats of a valued customer. The *mitron* also encouraged Guyot to eat as many as he could of the delicious cakes that always sat cooling on racks. To this the master baker turned a blind eye. In his first week, losses were heavy. Guyot thought all his Sundays had come at once. Soon enough, though, the warm, cloying waft of sugary chocolate and egg cooking in the afternoons had quite the opposite effect. Up to his elbows in the *plonge,* the sink full of buttery water with bobbing lemon halves where the utensils were washed, he lost his appetite. Though bread became his companion, something he couldn't be without, Guyot was never again tempted to gorge himself on cakes.

Halfway along one of the walls, another cellar leads off under the street. This is the *laboratoire,* the "laboratory" where the *pâtisseries* are made. There is a much smaller oven here, next to the *tour,* the block of marble set on a stainless steel rack and used for mixing dough. Numerous utensils hang from rails on the wall, and stainless steel basins of different sizes are stacked on the worktops. A digital scale sits next to piles of small iron molds, old, greasy, and black.

The kitchens and ovens of Parisian *boulangeries* are almost always located in the cellars, adjoining a subterranean, secret city of tunnels and sewers. The croissant, that French breakfast roll *par excellence,* was first made by bakers working at night, underground, during the siege of Budapest in 1686. Hearing the Turks tunneling under the city, they gave the alarm. To celebrate their victory, the bakers created pastries shaped in a crescent, the emblem of the Ottoman empire.

Morand, the pastry chef, won't arrive until dawn to bake the croissants he prepared the previous afternoon. Refrigerators hold the balls of dough and layers of pastry at temperatures that slow the process of fermentation. Everything will be ready for rolling and baking in the morning. It's no longer necessary to mix the dough at three o'clock in the morning in order for it to rise by six so that the loaves will come crackling and hissing out of the oven at seven.

Night work in *boulangeries* started under Napoleon III. Previously, baking was done in the morning and afternoon. People didn't expect hot, fresh bread and cakes first thing in the morning until they were given a taste for it by enterprising nineteenth-century *boulangers*. Refrigerators finally ended night work in the *boulangeries,* becoming the norm more than a decade ago. They helped to improve quality, because the longer the fermentation period, the less yeast one needs. Yeasts naturally present in the wheat have time to develop, giving a richer, more complex flavor.

Nevertheless, it was hard to break the nocturnal habit. Guyot was used to getting up in the night, having done so for twenty years. He still woke sometimes with the morning light in an anxious sweat, imagining that he had overslept and there was no bread: Customers bumped unexpectedly out of their morning routines were going to other *boulangeries* along the street, which would soon sell all they had baked, frustrating *their* customers. The disruption, aggravated by hunger, would put everybody in a bad mood. They would have to make do with yesterday's bread toasted instead of fresh *tartines,* baguettes halved, slit open, and spread with butter on the soft, warm crumb. The cafe would have no croissants piled in a basket on the zinc counter for customers to dunk in their morning coffee. There would be hell to pay. Guyot would be fired. . . .

Nowadays his chief anxiety is that the refrigerators might break down, allowing the dough to mushroom inside, pushing its way out the door. For that reason, he likes to arrive in good time for Sunday, and, assured that all is well, he works cheerfully as the city sleeps.

It takes about an hour for the oven to reach the right temperature and then baking can begin. There are 100 loaves of *pain de seigle* (rye bread) to be baked in small, oblong tins, 200 round loaves of *pain de campagne,* and 50 oval loaves of *pain au levain.* A large sourdough loaf, the *pain au levain* is a bread for

Baskets lined with jute cloth for baking loaves of *pain de campagne*.

connoisseurs and those who complain of digestive troubles. Though most people buy baguettes, there's pride for a baker in producing a good sourdough. (Mistrustful of the effect of the sealed refrigerators on the *levain,* the raising agent, Guyot allows his sourdough loaves to rise in the old storeroom off the cellar, where the air can reach them.) Then there are 50 loaves of *pain aux céréales,* made of wheat flour premixed with different stone-milled cereals, and 100 more loaves of *pain complet,* a whole-wheat loaf baked in the same oblong tins as the rye loaves. And there are the loaves of white bread: long, narrow baguettes; thinner, shorter *flûtes;* even smaller *ficelles,* plus *bâtards* that are half the length of a baguette and *pains* that are twice as large.

There are pastries to be made: *pains au raisin* and *pains chocolat; chaussons au pomme* (apple turnovers) and *palmiers,* the dry, heart-shaped flaky pastries; and croissants galore and at least two dozen brioches. The pastry chef will take care of them all. They have to be baked the morning they are sold; customers can get something baked, frozen, and reheated from a supermarket. The *pâtissier* will also be baking little almond tarts called *amandines* and tarts and *tartelettes* of all sizes and kinds—apple, pear, apricot, lemon, and cherry; custard tarts or flans with cherry and flans with prunes; apple doughnuts; five different kinds of éclair; rum babas; and, not to be forgotten, the 30 large *gâteaux,* including several savarins, some charlottes, quite a few *framboisiers* (made with a mousse of fresh raspberries), and the Black Forests and opéras—rectangular slabs of chocolate ganache layered with almond biscuit and coffee buttercream—that have been ordered during the week.

Guyot runs through this list in his mind as he gazes into the depths of the oven, looking for the rich glow on the walls at the back that means a firm crust for his loaves. Nothing special; it's an average Sunday. He takes from a refrigerator a basket of dough for country loaves called *pains de campagne* and begins cutting it into triangular portions. These he rounds into balls and, careful not to "break" the wheat—damaging the gluten by kneading too hard once it has started to rise—lifts them with cupped hands onto a tray.

From another refrigerator he takes a tray of rye loaves that have already been prepared. The dough has risen just enough to form a hump above the top of the tin. He slides the trays onto the shelves of a tall trolley. Once this is full, he wheels it over to the oven—and waits. The kneading has been mechanized; raising is overseen by timers, thermostats, and humidity gauges, but the act of putting the dough in the oven still depends on him. As an apprentice, it was the moment he felt the greatest apprehension: Had the dough risen sufficiently? Was the oven hot enough? The rising of the dough—caused by spores of yeast eating the sugars in the wheat—would be cut short by the fires of the oven. It took experience to tell if the dough had risen well. Baking bread is an empirical science; you have to have a nose for the weather, for the smell and the feel of the dough as you knead it. If there's a lot of humidity in the air, less water is necessary for the dough. But how much less? Once the balls of dough have gone into the oven, it's only a matter of taking out the baked loaves and leaving them to cool. From the look of the crust, a baker knows if his loaves are a success. And by the noise. Bread should "sing" as it comes out of the oven. The whistling sound of hot gases escaping through cracks in the crust tells the *boulanger* that his bread is properly cooked.

Guyot places tray after tray of large loaves into the oven until it's full but not crowded, as the larger loaves need more space. Eight trays in all, more than fifty loaves. The big two-pound loaves require a slow, rising heat. It's always better to bake with an oven that's getting hotter rather than cooling down, so they go in first. They cook gently, the heat working its way to their thick core as the oven temperature gradually increases.

By the time they are baked and ready to come out—about an hour—the *contre-maître,* the *ouvriers,* and the two apprentices have arrived. Guyot is the *maître,* the master baker in charge of the kitchens. The *contre-maître* is his foreman. He has two *ouvriers,* who are qualified journeyman bakers, and two apprentices. Morand, the pastry chef, a master *pâtissier-chocolatier-glacier,* has two *pâtissiers* under him. With the others there, the silence of the *fournil,* a nest of golden warmth in the darkness of the night, is broken by groans and jokes. The foreman complains about the dozy apprentices. In his haste, one of them sets a loaf upside down. The foreman is furious. "Are we expecting the undertaker today?" he cries. An upside-down loaf, facing hell rather than heaven, has always been a bad omen. Customers avoid them, as the loaf set aside for the public executioner used to be placed upside down.

Guyot helps to unload the first batch and load the next one. The large loaves sit like coals from the oven, glowing with moist, yellow warmth. Working fast so they won't have to wait for the heat to build up again, they hook out hot tins with iron rods and set the loaves in the oven with long wooden spades. Made of beech—wood that's hard, light, and fire-resistant—these spades are identical to those on the arms of the guild of *boulangers,* dating from before the thirteenth century. The *ouvriers* maneuver the long handles rapidly, coming near to clouting the apprentices as they turn. The space in front of the oven is a zone of concerted activity, a web of rapid, instinctive movements. For this reason, it's kept scrupulously clear. The bakers in their vests or stripped to the waist, eyes bright in the heat of the ovens, seem as though in a trance as they work. The banter soon gives way to silence again. There are no idle moments; not a motion is wasted. Like the tools, their gestures are part of ancient rituals. And so it continues until 6:00 A.M., by which time most of the special loaves have been baked and the baking of baguettes can commence.

O utside, the day is starting. A blade of clear, fresh light cuts along the Avenue Victor Hugo, reflected off the still-damp sidewalk. It augurs a perfect sunny day. By the time it's fully light, soon after six, Madame Benoit, the manager, arrives, wearing a white blouse and a printed silk scarf over her shoulders. Her first act is to place her purse under the counter. Then she summons Guyot by ringing a bell. An old voice tube still connects

Staff at Béchu preparing orders of *petit fours*.

the *fournil* with the shop, known as the *boutique*.

She wants to discuss the last-minute orders, the ones that always come late on Saturday afternoon for children's birthdays that have suddenly been remembered:

Madame Paujean has ordered three whole-wheat loaves, three ordinary rolls, and three whole wheat rolls.

Madame Gardot wants 22 *américaines*—long, light Viennese rolls suitable for hot dogs, probably for a children's party.

An apricot tart for four people has been ordered, without cream, for 11:00 A.M.

Another lady has left her telephone number in case her order, a *framboisier* for six people, can't be filled.

One customer wants 60 *navettes,* which are small Viennese rolls, two number-ones (a size of white bread), and 20 slices of *royale,* a sourdough. She is probably receiving guests.

Two *nattes,* plaited "country" loaves, have been ordered by Madame Bloch.

Madame Baudoin will be expecting one *framboisier,* one *feuillantine* (a kind of *millefeuille*), and 60 fresh petit fours, 30 sweet and 30 savory, for a reception at her home.

Once these orders have been confirmed, Madame Benoit replaces the speaking tube and takes up her position at the cash desk at the end of the counter. She stands on a raised dais, over a tray of coins hidden under the counter, counting them out into neat piles ready to give change from a thick glass dish in front of her. Change must never go from hand to hand. It must be laid out so any shortfall is evident, a reminder of the public's instinctive mistrust of bakers, though the scales once used to confirm the weight of a loaf as it was sold are now only decorative.

From her position directly opposite the main door, Madame Benoit can greet her staff as they arrive and dart behind her—giving a faint, deferential curtsy—to change into their black dresses and frilly pale pink aprons. By seven, Monsieur Amon, the *patron,* will be there, and will want to be assured that everything is ready.

The *boulangerie* on the Avenue Victor Hugo is called Béchu. Although there are five other *boulangeries* on the avenue and the surrounding streets, this one is special. For one thing, it doesn't say *"boulangerie"* outside, an omission that has impressed Roland Amon, the present owner, ever since he first saw Béchu. This morning, as nearly every morning, it gives him a little smile as he arrives. The absence of any trading description lends something indefinable. "People tell me I ought to add 'sandwiches' or whatever but I'm adding nothing. I like it. It's what fascinated me about this *boulangerie*."

Above the door is only the name of Béchu. When Madame Béchu had her premises redecorated after the Second World War, she felt there was no need to inform anybody of what was sold there. They already knew. She had become a legend in the sixteenth *arrondissement*. During the war, she fed the whole neighborhood with bread baked in the old oven that burned coal or wood. "She never gave up, she never stopped," says Roland Amon affectionately. "And she never sold on the black market. She sold her bread openly, for a fair price. People remembered that." Paris lives on bread, now as then. During times of famine, revolution, or siege, Parisians grudgingly ate *pain de Mme. de Montpensier,* made of oat flour if you were lucky, and sawdust, gravel, and husks if you weren't. At a very bad moment, in 1596, bones dug up from the cemeteries were ground and added. Parisians had eaten such fare again during the First World War, and the residents of Avenue Victor Hugo were grateful to Madame Béchu for not having had to eat it once more. After she had installed a new gas oven during the redecoration, there were those who complained the bread wasn't the same, but they still came every day.

Béchu is situated on a sharply angled corner opposite a newsstand, a bank, and a *brasserie* with an outside display piled high with ice, oysters, and shellfish. The window displays of Béchu are quite as they were in 1900, although it was called the Boulangerie Chevreau then. The only change is the name on the empty pale green and gold boxes of *confiseries,* each tied with a single pale pink lily made of paper and sugar, then carefully spaced on glass shelves. At the turn of the century there were thirty employees, including nine *triporteurs* who would set off along the avenue at six in the morning on their three-wheeled cycles with baskets full of bread and croissants, after the butlers of the neighborhood families had called to place their orders.

To one side of the corner double doors is a window filled with boxes of chocolate truffles from Angelina, the famous tearoom on the Rue de Rivoli, bottles of *marrons glacés* in kirsch, tins of Quality Street toffees from England, little transparent plastic sacks filled with homemade pink nougat and tied with pale green ribbon, boxes of fruit jellies, boiled sweets, and marzipan pigs. To the other side of the doors is a window full of tea tins and jars of blueberry and raspberry preserves for the breakfast table. The next window contains only packages of *biscottes,* dry toasts that were once made by the *boulanger.* The packages in the window at Béchu are from the firm of Roger in Aix-en-Provence, a little factory located next to a spring that provides the water used to make them. They're bought, for the most part, by grandmothers, a vestige of what was once a fashionable breakfast. In one corner of the window is the official *carte des prix des pains.* Once this was a legal requirement but nobody pays any notice now, and many of the plastic numbers indicating the prices have fallen off. Then comes the window full of *pâtisseries,* a regular detour for women walking their dogs, who approach with a secret smile that is reflected, with the leaves of the birch trees, in the glass.

The interior of the *boulangerie* was redecorated in 1936. The walls were painted champagne pink and the woodwork called forth in pale green, a color scheme that was refreshed in the 1950s. The *pâtisseries* are still displayed in a separate counter to the rear, next to the three little tables disposed in a row under the window. The tables create a *salon de thé,* a tearoom for the afternoons when the dumbwaiter hoists up trays of petit fours from the kitchen, with slips of paper corresponding to orders tucked under the rows of mini-éclairs and mini-choux with chocolate cream or mocha icing. On the shelves inside the shop are rows of transparent plastic boxes full of biscuits, and above them rows of champagne bottles, glinting in the champagne-pink light that spills from the Art Deco chandelier.

The theory of modern bakery layout is that the customer who wants a baguette should be ushered past the *pâtisseries* in a line formed in front of the display. The temptation is supposed to improve turnover, but Roland Amon is not sure that people want to be distracted while they buy their bread. And he would rather allow the prospective cake customer, who usually can't make up her mind, to savor the pleasure of doing so without feeling pressured by a line for bread.

In other ways, too, Béchu hasn't changed. The *maison* still takes special orders, the sign of a clientele that hasn't changed its ways. The assistants are already busy putting the special orders into boxes when the first customers arrive. Many are elderly, in the habit of rising early and of muttering a polite *"M'sieurdame"* to all and sundry as they enter the shop. Madame Benoit knows virtually all of the first few dozen customers by name, and the names of many more after that, having been there since 1963. She can remember when the loaves were weighed in the scales before they were sold; if the weight was short, she gave change in sweets or cakes.

Although it's a pleasant morning, and a Sunday, the customers appear anxious. The line, which seems to be perpetually at least seven persons long, provides opportunity for neighborly exchange, but once near the counter, people grow quiet. There is ample bread for all, but their faces become grim and they fall silent as they survey the loaves lined up on racks behind the assistant. They all want a baguette that is "well cooked but not *too* well cooked," a perfect baguette in other words, and despite their trust in Béchu, they seem to fear they will be given a loaf left over from yesterday, or one that is not properly baked. There's a flicker of hunger, too, across their faces—an ancient, distracting feeling. They don't look at the assistant serving them but run flinty eyes over the bread. The transaction is serious and hurried.

For a brief second the line thins, and only an old man is left at the counter. One of the two assistants profits from the pause to gather up the few baguettes remaining in the basket and place them on the shelf.

Downstairs in the *fournil,* the oven is good and hot, and full of baguettes. A second batch is ready to go in: lengths of dough lined on a canvas stretcher. Guyot leans over them, making the characteristic diagonal slashes on the surface with his cutthroat razor. The slashes are like a signature to another baker. They are Guyot's only physical contribution to the baking process.

A machine kneads the dough, another machine rolls it out, and—once he has made the slashes to prevent the baguette from twisting and tearing apart from the tremendous force of the gases expanding inside—another machine loads it into the oven. More than 1,500 baguettes will be baked that day, in several batches. Many customers will return at least once to buy a second baguette for lunch. Some will come back a third time, to buy one for dinner.

A long stick with a crust so sharp it can cut the roof of your mouth and a crumb so light it hardly exists, the baguette is the resolution of desires: the perfect balance of crumb and crust, of sweet and salty. It contains only wheat and water, yet it took a thousand years to bake. In three hours it's gone, either eaten or too hard and dry to be worth eating. It always leaves you satisfied, but not stuffed, and eager to eat another as soon as hunger returns. Although it became common only after the Second World War, nobody can say who first baked it or named it.

The history of the baguette is the history of France. Paris sits on the crest of a wide plain of wheat fields, an enormous granary hundreds of miles around. There is Picardie, where Van Gogh painted the waving crops (and was driven mad by the impossibility of capturing their golden harvest yellow). There's Brie, also

The quintessential French loaf, the baguette took
a thousand years to perfect, and goes dry after three hours.
Every day, the French eat $1^{1/4}$ baguettes each. They used to eat two.

known for its cheese, and the Beauce, between Paris and Orléans, where highwaymen plagued the long, lonely roads. Wheat requires the best land, but in return will sustain a large population. Wheat, made into bread, is the basic foodstuff of Parisians—and of the French—who eat 1¼ baguettes each per day. Consumption has declined drastically since the Second World War when they ate two baguettes each, and a century before that when they each ate the equivalent of three.

Wheat is also a staple food of the Italians (who make it into pasta), the British, and the Germans. The bread eaten by their descendants in the United States derives from the Anglo-Saxon tradition, which differs from the French. In beer-drinking northern Europe, brewer's yeast was more widely used, and bread was made from a variety of cereals. Rye and barley, hardy grains that grew where wheat until recently would not, were common. Bread made and leavened with wheat flour was a luxury enjoyed by the French.

To make wheat into bread it must first be milled. Until the twentieth century, milling in France was a long, sorry history of exploitation and disaster. It was a *droit de seigneur,* a privilege of the local lord. In addition to paying a fee to the miller, usually in grain, peasants who took their wheat to be milled paid a tax to the feudal lord on whose land that mill stood. Powered by water, mills came to a halt if the river dried up, or worse, caught fire if it flowed too fast: The millstones could spark and ignite the timber frames, and there was nothing to be done after that except call the charred ruins the *Moulin Brulé,* the Burnt Mill, a place name still common and remembered with sorrow. Bread shortages were common. Until the nineteenth century, the wheat crop would fail once or twice a decade, causing deprivation and famine. At these times, millers were often accused of hoarding wheat to drive prices up. Over the centuries many were jailed, mobbed, and even hanged.

Windmills, introduced from Asia after the Crusades, were little better; idle without wind, they also required careful setting of the sails to prevent the millstones from turning too fast and tearing up the grains.

But a plentiful harvest meant survival and prosperity, and for the miller or grain merchant, a chance to spend the money made in the bad years. Loose money lured women to these out-of-town places. The innocent windmill perched on the hill was thus a sight that struck terror when it was still but it became a place of gaiety and folly when the sails resumed turning. An early Impressionist masterpiece, *Moulin de la Gallette,* depicts an old windmill that had been transported in 1834 to the hills of Montmartre from its place of origin near the Palais Royal, where it had turned since the thirteenth century. It became the site of the Sunday afternoon dances painted by Renoir. The most famous cabaret in Paris, the Moulin Rouge, was so named to evoke for the Parisians who had come from the fields to work in the factories the ruddy, bucolic pleasures of drinking wine and eating rye-flour galettes—not to mention gambling, brawling, taking a turn with and perhaps even marrying the wealthy miller's daughter.

The flour from these mills was coarse and brown for the most part. Sifting it yielded *fleur de farine,* the "flower" of the milled grain, which was fine and white. (Our word *flour* comes from this source.) Even ground by the best stone wheels—hard, rough burrs extracted from the hillsides of the Marne valley to the east of Paris, with faces cross-cut in a precise pattern—less than a fifth of the flour that resulted was fine, white *fleur.* Most days, if you were a farmer or a tradesman, your bread had a brown or gray crumb, with a rough, gritty texture and hard, black crust. Made with an average grade of wheat, it was nonetheless nutritious and remained fresh for days. But bread made with *fleur de farine* was special. Dainty, light white bread was a staple of the rich. The crust was golden—signifying opulence—and the crumb was a buttery yellow white that didn't retain moisture, so it had to be eaten promptly. Such indulgence was a mark of privilege.

As long ago as the thirteenth century, the preference was noted of Parisians—who have always had *le goût du luxe*—for white bread. In those days and for another six centuries, the best white bread, made with brewer's yeast, came from the village of Gonesse, now under the flight path of the Roissy airport runways.

Now there is little left to recall its illustrious past except old stone-fronted mansions sited with evident pomp. Wheat fields still crown the surrounding hills, crowded with ears that have been growing there for more than a millennium. Bakers from Gonesse brought their bread to the Paris markets twice a week. It was the whitest, the lightest, and the dearest, but they always trundled home with empty carts.

Since that time, control over the price and quality of bread had been sought by a long succession of edicts, both royal and Republican. The point of these decrees was to ensure that a good-sized, nutritious, affordable loaf was available to all. Bad farming, terrible harvests, catastrophic housekeeping, and a burgeoning, hungry urban population finally brought on the Revolution. Like the peasants who resented the miller on whom they depended, the rabble of Paris loathed the baker, who either had no bread when wheat was scarce or, if he did, charged dearly for it. Louis XVI, Marie-Antoinette, and their son were nicknamed the *boulanger,* the *boulangère,* and the baker's boy by the women who went to bring them from Versailles to face the guillotine. A humble *boulanger* named Denis Francois was lynched in October 1789 by a hungry Paris mob outraged at the high price of his bread. They accused him of hoarding, though it turned out that he had merely been passing on the cost of flour to his customers.

Once *boulangers* no longer had to fear their starving customers, they could apply themselves to improving their bread. Because price and weight were fixed, only by baking a better loaf could they increase trade and profit. But it would be another century before the marvellous baguette—whose name means "wand"—came into being.

Before anyone could bake a baguette, however, brewer's yeast was required. Though *boulangers* did bake some bread leavened with brewer's yeast, such as those at Gonesse, it was more typical of eastern Europe. In 1840 a Prussian officer named Zang guessed that Parisians would like the light loaves of his homeland. He imported wheat flour from Hungary, hired bakers from Vienna, and opened for business in the Rue de Richelieu, selling loaves with a fine, white crumb that were "long rather than large," according to one account.

His loaves were a luxury, requiring skill to control the rising. Brewer's yeast was fragile, and expensive, until 1872, when the Hungarian industrialist Baron Springer opened a factory in the suburbs of Paris to produce the dry, powdered brand still widely used today. Fine white flour was costly, too, until steam-driven, metal-roller mills replaced stone mills. By sifting out the finely milled wheat and passing the remainder through heavier rollers, three-quarters of the grain could be recovered as white flour. Mechanical mixing bowls replaced the old *pétrins,* the long V-shaped, wooden kneading troughs, and a new type of oven, based on a Viennese design, became common. It had steam injectors to keep the crust moist as the loaves baked so that they could expand easily. But still, as the new century began, there were no baguettes.

A Parisian wine merchant who also sold sandwiches asked his baker to make his long *pains* longer, and longer still, so he could cut more sandwiches from them. These loaves became known as *marchands de vin.* Attesting to their origin, in the *Musée du Pain* at Charenton in the suburbs of Paris, is a basket six feet long from the 1920s, in which the dough was left to rise and the loaf to cool afterward. In a guide to French bread published in Switzerland in the 1930s, long, narrow loaves made with brewer's yeast are illustrated. "In Paris," notes the author, "they're called Noels, Lemardeleys or Richelieus, the names of fashionable restaurants." In the countryside, they were called *flûtes,* but nobody in rural France ate white bread often before the Second World War. In fact, it was customary to ask anybody with a *flûte* if someone was sick at home. White bread was a treat, easy to digest. After the war, though, all of a sudden baguettes were everywhere. People were tired of eating gray or black bread; they wanted white.

The name of the first baker to call his long loaves baguettes is not known. Baguettes are made from French wheat—a "soft" grade, in which the elastic gluten is intact after milling, with some Canadian Manitoba added—mixed with water at the right temperature, kneaded, and left to rise a few hours, then formed into long rolls and cut with sharp, even incisions across the top just before being put into a very hot oven fitted with a vapor device. A small amount of salt is added to the dough, and there is some in the wheat itself. Any additive apart from ascorbic acid—vitamin C, which helps rising and is destroyed in cooking—is illegal, as is flour whitened by the bleaching process used in Britain and America. No preservatives are used. There's no need for them. Who would want to forgo the taste of a fresh baguette?

B y midday, Béchu has already sold all of its morning baguettes, and the first of the lunchtime batch arrives from the ovens, their fresh brown and gold crusts still cracking in the basket. Outside, the street is busy with shoppers buying meat for Sunday lunch from the butcher and cheeses from the *crémerie.* The *boulangerie* is the hub of all this activity. The other shopkeepers always ask Roland Amon when he is closing for his holidays; they time theirs to coincide because they know that with the *boulangerie* shut, people will go elsewhere and the *quartier* will be deserted.

Midday is the moment for Roland to step out into the street with a long metal handle to roll out the awnings, colored by the afternoon sun a parched pink and green. Then he takes over as usual from Madame

Removing paper used to screen the sun from the windows at Béchu.

Benoit at the cash desk. Roland, in his early fifties, has a baker's creamy white pall to his complexion. It's as if he can never quite get the flour out of his pores, though it isn't often now that he labors in the kitchen. He enjoys the midday rush: the bundles of baguettes and the avalanche of coins.

Roland Amon grew up in a village outside Paris. In the 1950s the region was still rural, but now has become part of the ever-growing suburbs that spread between the industrial zone of Melun and the peaceful royal gardens of Fontainebleau.

Roland's grandfather had a farm. The family had been there since the Revolution and probably much before that. No one knows because it was the *curé,* the priest, who had kept the parish records and they vanished with him, thrown into the Seine by an anticlerical mob. The family members were smallholders, "simple people," says Roland. His father, who was the third of four sons, found life on the farm arduous. They woke at four in the morning to milk the cows. For dinner, they ate soup with chunks of brown, chewy bread floating in it. Twice a week, on Tuesdays and Saturdays, the *boulanger* came five miles from the village to deliver bread to the local farms, his blue Peugeot van touring the narrow lanes and crossing the fields, loaded with loaves. But the *boulanger* also owned a black Citroën, called a *Traction-avant.* It was a prestige car, driven by prosperous businessmen and government officials. The mayor had one; so did Cochin, the *boulanger,* whom Roland's father used to see riding with his family on Sunday afternoons.

"My father was fascinated by this car," recalls Roland. "It was 1936 when he first saw it; there weren't many then. Twenty years later he finally bought one himself!"

The car confirmed to Roland's father that being a *boulanger* was preferable to life on the farm, and so Cochin was prevailed upon to take him as an apprentice. Roland's father was fourteen years old, accustomed to hard work and rising early, the ideal dough out of which to form a baker. There was no money exchanged, though from time to time his mother put a little bottle of Calvados in his lunch box, for the *patron*. His apprenticeship lasted two years. Afterwards, he found a place with another *boulanger*. It would be a long time before he could afford that Citroën; he had to give all his earnings to his mother.

Then Roland's father was called up for military service. It was during the Occupation, but he didn't want to work for the Nazis—the Vichy government sent French conscripts to German factories—so he ran away. He hid in the mountains of Auvergne, making bread in old communal stone ovens still intact in the remote villages. After the war he returned and met Roland's mother. "She was also from the land," says Roland. "Her grandfather was a *vigneron*," a vintner. For a while, Roland's father worked for a *boulanger* at Melun who opened at 5:30 A.M. and had a stock of coffee under the counter, rations procured with an army card. Then, with some savings and a small dowry from his wife, he started looking for his own premises.

On sunny Sundays, after lunch at the farm, Roland's father used to swim with his friends in the Seine, at a village called Seineport, afterwards buying brioches from a baker near the old jetty. He was sentimental about this *boulangerie* and made an offer, but the owner didn't want to sell, so Roland's father bought other premises, a small *affaire* near Nemours, and commenced business. Roland was born the following year, and a year later the baker at Seineport decided to sell. He demanded a steep price, but Roland's father wanted the little country *boulangerie* near the old jetty. It was 1947 when they moved in. There were pigs in the yard and rats sometimes took refuge in the cellar when the waters of the Seine rose too high.

The pigs were not an unusual part of the commercial property of a *boulanger*. Country bakers kept them, and so did many urban ones, to eat the bran left over after the wheat had been milled and sifted. The farmers who were the main customers of Roland's father regarded the nutritious bran as fit only for pigs: They wanted bread made with fine white flour. But the pigs were happy and, in due course, became fine hams and pâtés to accompany the bread that Roland's father baked. The rats were a nuisance, however. They lived on the flotsam washed up by the barges, and they tried to get at the flour. The solution was to keep a cat. Before the posting of a certificate of hygiene near the entrance became a requirement, the sign of a well-kept *boulangerie* was a cat dozing in the window under blinds drawn against the afternoon sun.

Two more children came, brothers to Roland, born a year apart. "I used to work with them and my father. We were always alongside him. We made tarts with him. We lived in two rooms so we were always in the *fournil*. We played football in there, did our homework there, everything." Without really noticing it, Roland became an apprentice to his father at fourteen, the same age his father had been. He was reluctant, however. He had seen his mother kneading the choux pastry all day and his father always at the oven. But Roland would become a *boulanger* because he was the eldest son. He was also the shame of the family in his father's view, because of his poor spelling. His brother Gilles, on the other hand, was a bright pupil with an aptitude for numbers. He would become a *pâtissier,* a scientific profession with greater prospects of reward. The third brother, the youngest, was allowed to do what he pleased.

"My father was brought up by my grandfather, who was a very hard man," Roland recounts. "They were marked by certain things in their youth and they thought life was like that; and it would be like that for their children and grandchildren. They had no idea that Voltaire had said man needs the three eights: eight hours of sleep followed by eight hours of work, followed by eight hours of leisure. This, in the eighteenth century! In a *boulangerie,* it's still twelve-hour days.

"His moral assumptions hadn't been altered by the little schooling he received. I don't think he was very happy, finally, because the *boulangerie* eventually became a sufference. It was hard for him. He wasn't enough of a businessman. The big problem with a *boulangerie,* especially nowadays, is that you have to be more of a shopkeeper than an artisan. If you're only an artisan, no matter how good you are, it will be hard for you. We live in a commercial society. Even in the 1960s, it was already like that. And my mother wasn't very good at commerce either. In a couple, there should always be one who's ambitious. Neither one of them was.

"They had met through a kind of arrangement. My grandfather had four sons; that meant four sons to marry. It was like that . . . There were two things that were never talked about at the house: sex and money. Never did I hear those things discussed. If I'm with my brother Gilles now, an hour wouldn't pass when we didn't talk about money. We talk about it all the time. Ours is a profession where everything is based on money. The fascination of big *affaires* is the problem of turnover. Everybody talks about that. In my father's bakery nobody talked about money. And sex was never mentioned."

The family was Catholic, though like the families of all *boulangers,* they postponed the Lord's day— indefinitely. Secular needs were more urgent than spiritual ones, a point implicitly acknowledged in the biblical warning that man cannot live by bread alone.

Roland's father mistrusted the *curé.* Because he was working, he never heard the sermons and saw only the looks on the faces of the congregation as they crossed the square to his bakery after Mass. He vaguely resented it when the *curé* came to bless the bread at Easter; it gave the *curé* an obscure advantage. There was a kind of unmarked commercial division between them. They had the same customers after all, who each Sunday went from the premises of one to the other. The priest suspected that the smells from the bakery distracted the congregation. The baker, in other words, was a rival. People ate his bread every day and the materiality of the baker's communion with his customers frustrated the *curé*. It was a metaphor yet real, a ritual that didn't need to represent anything. The fact that Roland's father never went to church was also an affront.

Roland's father would have been surprised to learn of this rivalry. "He never went to Mass because he was working on Sunday, like all *boulangers*. I've never seen a *boulanger* at a church on Sunday, never. It's the busiest day, especially in the country. They might go on other days of the week, but never on Sunday."

By Monday Roland's father was too tired to go to Mass. On Tuesday the week began again. "I was a choirboy and he used to say I was going to the church to avoid working," said Roland. "That was the rapport he had with religion. It didn't run very deep." According to Roland, the most important people in the village were the *curé,* the doctor, and the baker. People were proud to have a good baker. "The *boulanger* would be excused everything if he made good bread. If he made average bread, he would be esteemed, but there was a great respect for a good baker. It was his bread that you ate every day. My father was a notable in the village. It was something that was very important to him, that he had but I don't."

Now there is more choice, of course, and people can easily make a detour to the next bakery, or the next village. Before, if the local *boulanger* was less than average, the village might seem to shun itself. The café would fill up, and the café owner, who perhaps could get his bread from elsewhere, would be prevailed upon to sell a loaf or two. That was usually the beginning of the end. . . .

To create a French village, you needed first of all a church and a *boulangerie*. All the rest would follow, but without the *curé* and the *boulanger,* the community wouldn't exist. There would be no need for a mayor or a doctor. The villagers could forgo political, medical, and even spiritual services, but not their daily bread. Bread was life.

And so the *curé* was always cordial with the *boulanger,* and ate his bread every day, too.

oland was seventeen when he finished his apprenticeship with his father. He took the practical exam to earn his *Certificat d'aptitude professionnel* at the École de Boulangerie in Paris, looking out the window at the great mill next to the school, seven stories high, that hummed and rattled all night and all day long. There was a written test and a practical one. He was given the materials and had to make bread and cakes —everything you would expect to find if you entered a *boulangerie* at seven in the morning. He received the second highest grade.

Roland immediately went back to work for his father, but there was an argument and he left for Paris. "I worked three months here, six months there, a year somewhere else. I went to places to learn and once I learned I got bored. It was more romantic than that. I worked nights, so when I made a bit of money I left. . . ."

One of his *patrons* was Monsieur Meurice, who was sixty years old and spoke in a brusque Parisian argot. His bakery in the Rue Rambuteau was always busy. At that time, the 1960s, the great food markets that Zola called the belly of Paris were still operating there under the wrought-iron Baltard pavilions. And because the *fournil* was at street level behind the *boutique*, Roland was able to observe the business of the night. Every Sunday, after the bakery closed, he would go with the apprentice and Monsieur Meurice for aperitifs at each of the bistros they supplied. And then they would finally sleep.

"It was an education for me because he was someone who wouldn't let anything pass. I remember one day he told me off because I'd made the dough a bit hard and the *ficelles* were curved. If the dough is too stiff, the baguette is twisted. He made a fuss. And he did a thing I still do: He often weighed the *viennoiserie*. It's the sign of a real professional. You take a croissant and weigh it. It mustn't weigh more than forty-five grams. If it weighs sixty, you're losing money. If it weighs thirty, you're losing customers. He would pass by, weigh them, and come back to tell us off. It's stayed with me, and I'm a bit like that."

When Roland was a journeyman baker, one of his *patrons* was Victor Baudouin, who earlier had presented him with his professional diploma. Roland used to see him arrive at work in a Mercedes, wearing a white shirt. It was the late 1960s, and the glamour of being a baker was not great. They weren't known as artisan-bakers then; they were *ouvriers,* manual workers. "You didn't have much pull with girls," he said. "They wanted to marry men in advertising. I never told people I was a *boulanger.* I would be introduced as a *boulanger* by others because it was a bit folkloric. It was charming. How I suffered!" Victor Baudouin gave Roland a taste for *belles affaires,* bakeries that are well placed. "It's a profession like any other. The ability to make bread, even good bread, isn't enough. You have to be ambitious. You have to be commercial." Baudouin understood the commercial parameters of running a successful *boulangerie.* "He wasn't a great baker but he had two of the busiest *boulangeries* in Paris." Both were opposite railway stations. The passing trade—which by the 1960s was in too much of a hurry for lunch and eager to be sold sandwiches and savories—was phenomenal.

Until the 1920s when they started selling *pâtisserie,* bakers never became very wealthy. The profession was respected and it was stable, but *boulangers* only prospered when they started baking cakes, and later, selling sandwiches. "Nowadays, it's a profession in which we're both traders and artisans, and some bakers are more like traders. They buy concerns and augment the turnover so they can sell at a profit. Others are still artisans. They buy a bakery not because it's well placed but because it's convenient or suitable for them. And bakers like that eventually look around and feel dismayed because they see that the trader has done better financially."

Roland Amon, counting the avalanche of change at Béchu.
"It's a profession like any other," he says. "The ability to bake bread,
even good bread, isn't enough."

At half past one the butcher and the *crémerie* close. The *brasserie* is full and people wait at the bar for tables. At Béchu the midday rush has slowed and there are no baguettes left, causing evident disappointment to hurried customers in a last-minute search for one. They settle reluctantly for a richer *pain de campagne* or a *pain,* exactly the same as a baguette but larger and with more crumb.

Downstairs in the *fournil,* activity has slowed. Guyot has left with the foreman for an aperitif at a bar along the street, leaving the *sous-maître* and one of the apprentices to put more batches of baguette dough to rise in the refrigerators, before they too leave. The other apprentice will return with the foreman later to bake them. The *pâtissier* is also present, putting the last decorative touches on the large *gâteaux* ordered for the afternoon. In the shop upstairs there is a lull. During the week, Béchu is busy throughout the day selling sandwiches to local shop and office workers. On Sunday few customers show up until later in the afternoon. Roland has gone for lunch at the *brasserie.* Madame Benoit has returned to her post at the till and is sorting piles of coins.

Although Madame Benoit is not married to Roland—he is a confirmed bachelor—hers is an essential role at Béchu, that of the wife of the *boulanger.* Indeed, she is the wife of a *boulanger,* but he works elsewhere. She is also the daughter of one. Her mother was the wife of a *boulanger,* too. It's a role she understands.

A famous engraving from the fifteenth century shows a *boulangerie* within a walled court. Standing in front is the town baker, looking healthy and prosperous and carrying a jug, perhaps to fetch water for baking. The *boulangerie* is a small, narrow house. A window opens to the street at ground level, and presumably the oven is below in the cellar. Above this window is the ledge on which the *boules* are set, in an open arch lined with shelves. (From these simple round loaves the *boulanger*—the maker of *boules*—gets his name.) Next to the arch with the loaves is a door from which the *boulanger's* wife is peering out, one eye on her husband.

The *boulanger's* wife—who always had bread to eat and money in her apron pocket—was a figure of envy. She shared in the respect accorded her husband, and he was out of her hair, working long hours down in the *fournil*. As the queen of her *boutique,* she held court unhindered. She knew everybody, saw them every day, and heard all the gossip. The *boulangerie* was to women—who brought tarts they had prepared at home to cook in the baker's oven—what the café was to men.

But she also excited among men a certain desire, with her creamy, wheaten skin and well-fed figure. The forms and dimensions of the wares she sold naturally gave rise to ribaldry. And there was always the suspicion that her husband—purple from kneading and bleary-eyed from lack of sleep—spent too many nights tending his oven and not enough attending to his wife. In popular myth, the *boulanger* was a likely cuckold.

This was the premise of one of the most cherished prewar French films, *La femme du boulanger,* adapted by Marcel Pagnol from a story by Jean Giono. In Giono's tale of life in rural Provence, the wife of the *boulanger* runs off with a shepherd. The poor, distraught baker loses the strength to knead the dough, and his bread becomes soft and tasteless, to the consternation of the entire village. It smells suspiciously of anise, arousing the curiosity and delight of the local children, after he falls asleep over the *pétrin* drunk on Pastis, the spirit made from anise. Finally, there is no bread at all; the *boulangerie* is closed. The villagers wonder what will become of them. "A village without bread, what's that?" asks one. "Waste your time, exhaust the animals going to fetch bread from the next village? And worse. Where will we take the flour from the next harvest? If the *boulanger* doesn't get a hold of himself, it'll mean selling your flour to a merchant, and then going to buy your bread money in hand." The only thing that will save the *boulanger,* and the villagers' daily bread, is the return of his wife, Aurélie. She, meanwhile, has begun to find the charms of the shepherd a bit too rustic. Told of the sorry state of her husband, and of the village, she finally decides to return. The *boulanger* promises not to neglect her in the future but goes straight back to work. The village suddenly forgets its scorn for Aurélie, who injured the baker's heart and their stomachs, and rejoices to hear again "the oven purring and grumbling in the night."

The villagers in Giono's tale, written in the 1920s, still reaped their own wheat and took it to the miller to be ground and sifted, then deposited the flour with the *boulanger,* who baked it into loaves for them. A tally was kept on sticks. The *boulanger* had one and the farmer had another. For each transaction the two sticks were aligned and knicked with a knife. Farmers didn't pay for their bread with money; they bartered wheat for it. France was a nation of small farmers until very recently; the *boulanger*'s tallying sticks were common, and the complaints of the villagers in Giono's story were many centuries old. Selling to a merchant meant accepting his price. It was a loss of status for the farmer, who feared exploitation. The exchange with the *boulanger,* who took some of the farmer's flour to bake and sell for his own account, was more equitable, and it was part of the intimacy that existed between the baker and the locals.

If bread was life, wheat was money. The slang word for money in French is *blé,* which means wheat. The farmer and the miller could both hope to accumulate *blé* or money, the farmer if the crop was good, the miller (who had stored away his share from milling everybody's wheat) if the crop failed. Barter worked in the villages, but in towns, *boulangers* had to buy their wheat from the mills, and if the *boulanger* couldn't pay at once, the mills extended credit. In this way, millers became the middlemen and financiers of *boulangeries,* which they still are. Their representatives tour the bakeries, peddling new types of flour. They make the acquaintance of all the bakers and their wives, plus their children and their apprentices. They know if a bakery is busy because they know how much flour is used, and whether the baker is good. Once he has worked his way up to foreman and then master baker, a good baker might start looking around for an *affaire* of his own. The mill representative, a garrulous fellow with many contacts, knows who is thinking of selling and how much a business is worth. He can bring together the enterprising, diligent young baker, the retiring master baker with a business for sale, and possible sources of finance, such as the mill. But there will be one thing he will want to be sure of first: the wife of the *boulanger.*

Ideally, she will be someone from the *métier,* either the daughter of a baker or someone who has worked in a *boulangerie.* That way, she will be accustomed to the hours and the deprivations. Often the young baker's heart is won over by a new salesgirl; romance blooms, there is a *gâteau de marriage,* and pretty soon, a *brioche dans le four,* literally a "bun in the oven." This is what happened to the parents of Madame Benoit.

The wife of the boulanger has duties as strict and onerous as those of her husband. She must be pleasant and outgoing, for no one will buy bread from a shrew. She must have good business sense because she's in charge of the cash. She must be prepared to work long hours like her husband. The mill representatives have seen it go wrong, after all: the baker glaring in fury into the oven, his wife abandoning the *boutique.* They know that the key to a thriving *boulangerie* is the wife.

Uncle Farine—his real name is Lefevre, but everyone knows him as Uncle Farine—was the mill representative who mentioned to Roland that a *boulangerie* of some importance, the likes of which there are only a handful in Paris, might be coming up for sale.

Figures like Uncle Farine used to be known as *rouleurs,* or wheelers, around whom the bakery business turns. In the old days, they could be recognized by their gold-tipped canes with hollow shafts for inserting in sacks of flour and extracting samples, and by the blue and white ribbons they wore during the annual parade of the guild of *boulangers*. These days, *rouleurs* carry cellular phones.

Roland had asked Uncle Farine if there were any interesting *affaires* coming up. At the time he was back at the family bakery at Seineport, where he had tripled the turnover. His brother Gilles, who, as their father had wished, had gotten his *brevet*—his diploma as a *pâtissier*—as well as a degree in economics, was working in management for a computer firm. "You know," he told Roland, "computers are like the steel industry. One day there's going to be a lot of unemployment. . . . " Cakes were different. To the chagrin of Gilles's wife, for whom cakes had less cachet than computers, Gilles decided to return to the *laboratoire,* and with Roland was looking for the right opportunity.

There was an *affaire* near the Champs Elysées, but it was sold the next day. Then Uncle Farine mentioned Béchu. Madame Ardel was the owner. (The wives of *boulangers* become the widows of *boulangers,* well known from a popular rhyme for their riches.) Her late husband had bought it from the heirs of Madame Béchu. *"Affaires* of this caliber, they're coveted, they're sold before they're sold! I said I'd buy it right away," said Roland. His brother came in as a partner. "He stayed with me for two years and then he went to Avenue Mozart where he's like a fish in water. It's his natural element. He's a *pâtissier,* despite his economics degree. That's what he always will be."

✷

Throughout the afternoon there is a steady flow of customers pulling up in cars, strolling into Béchu, and emerging with boxes tied with ribbon dangling from their fingers. Most are men, fathers or sons, no doubt (for husbands and lovers, the florist remains open two doors away). The continental habit of

The wood-burning oven in the basement of the Moulin de la Vierge, Paris.
Long wooden spades are used to place the loaves.

bringing *gâteaux* to gatherings of family or close friends has allowed *pâtisserie* to thrive. There just would not be the same sighs for a frozen cake.

Roland watches with approval the charlottes, operas, and *framboisiers* going into the cardboard boxes. "A good *gâteau* you remember," he says. "It's rare. Curiously, *pâtisserie* is more tarnished than bread. Often things aren't really fresh, or they're too cold. Refrigeration has killed a kind of spontaneity in *pâtisserie*. Because there's nothing more simple in the world, really. You take sugar and milk, mix flour with eggs and butter. Then you put some fresh fruit on it, a little *crème pâtissière,* and you have a treat! Some jam on your fresh strawberries and you're in paradise! So why aren't they good? Because the *boulanger* who has become a *pâtissier* will use strawberries that he's had in the fridge, a base that he's had for a while, as stiff as cardboard, and he'll use just any type of butter, or none at all. There are varieties of butter and even varieties of sugar. It's the basic ingredients that make the difference. When you find something made the same day, from the best ingredients, it's unforgettable! It's a rule that if you pass at eight in the morning and see a window that's already full of cakes, don't buy there, because they were made the day before."

He prefers to leave Madame Benoit to deal with the *pâtisseries*. He feels that taking care of customers requires patience and tact. "Look at that monsieur, for example. He won't trouble himself. He'll buy two baguettes. But madame there, she wants a cake, but she doesn't know which. It'll take a while.... 'What's in this? What's that made with?' When it comes to *pâtisserie,* everything changes. A cake is expensive and it's not something you buy every day, so you want to take your time. But bread is cheap, and it's something you buy every day."

In fact, as far as Roland is concerned, bread is too cheap.

"It's a very rich source of nutrition, very good for you, that requires a lot of work. In 1960 it cost the same price as a newspaper or a postage stamp. All those things now cost more than a baguette, but no matter, when the price of a baguette goes up, you get roasted! You aren't pardoned. It costs three francs eighty [about seventy-six cents], which is really nothing. You wouldn't even dare to leave that as a tip in a restaurant! Even here in a wealthy neighborhood, when it comes to bread, you have complete solidarity between the *grande bourgeoisie* and the proletariat! A *concorde*. It always was like that. In my father's day, it was the same. If you interfere with their daily bread, you'd better beware!"

The blinds are lowered fully against the afternoon sun, though there is nothing left in the window to protect other than an assortment of some of the odd things that languish in the windows of all *boulangeries:* biscuits, sweets, artificial flowers, plastic toys, corn dolls, sheaves of wheat, and decorative plaited loaves that seem old enough to be religious relics, which, in a way, they are. Before Christian times, widows used to cut their plaits and throw them on their husbands' funeral pyres. Plaited loaves were a token of grief.

The cakes have nearly all been sold and the *pâtissier* has gone home. A fresh batch of baguettes has come up and waits in a basket, anticipating the stir that has begun in the neighborhood. More baguettes will be sold in the hours between five and seven than at lunchtime, as families return from a day out or a weekend away, and remember that there's nothing in the fridge. As long as there's a baguette, nobody goes hungry, nobody complains as they do their homework or watch the evening news.

With some ham or cheese, the baguette makes a meal. A meal in France is a number of dishes accompanied by bread. Between courses, the French eat bread; between mouthfuls, they eat bread. They break off chunks of it with their hands, allowing the crumbs to fall directly onto the table, or tablecloth. (In the best restaurants—serving many foreign diners—side plates are now provided.) But there is no slovenliness in littering the table with crumbs, rather a great reverence, evidence that bread is more essential than anything on a plate. The French quickly discern which bread they prefer and make wide detours, even for something as apparently standardized as a baguette. "A real *boulanger* has a personal characteristic," says Roland. "I like bread that's quite well cooked and crusty. I'm going to make bread to my taste. And after a while I'll have a clientele with the same taste as me. In a supermarket or a *boulangerie* where the *patron* doesn't make the bread, they bake a uniform loaf. People come to buy their bread at least once a day, sometimes twice or three times, so it doesn't take long for them to acquire an affinity for what you do, as long as it's made by hand."

It doesn't seem like an inconvenience for those who stand in the line at Béchu for the third time that day. They wait with the same air of half-starved anticipation, and are equally concerned about which baguette they receive. The last customers, who arrive too late for the remaining loaves, look fretful and worried, and dash out to make frantic tours of the area looking for a *boulangerie* that hasn't sold out.

But by seven-thirty, all of them have. All over Paris, and throughout France, it's the same. At Béchu, it's time to draw in the awnings, sweep away the crumbs, and count the last of the coins.

Parmentier, the eighteenth-century French agronomist who took an enlightened interest in bread, admitted that the history of baking is "highly obscure." It may be that, like other primitive peoples, the Gauls began by chewing grains of wheat whole. Parmentier speculated that "the grinding of the teeth suggested the action of a mill, and the mixture of wheat and saliva produced a dough."

On the other hand, they might have been taught by the Phoenicians, who founded the French city of Marseille. The Phoenicians had learned from the Egyptians, who raised wheat—mankind's first major crop—in handsome, orderly cultivations. The Egyptians knew how to make leaven from fruit cultures

At the Moulin de la Vierge, Paris, a pupil from a neighborhood *lycée*
buys a *pain chocolat* on her way home.

(fermenting matter they also used in mummification) and recovered yeast from beer, of which they were great drinkers. At any rate, the Gauls—whose name derives from a Celtic word meaning cultivated land—were already baking bread when the Romans arrived with their bakers, who had learned from the Greeks the recipes for thirty types of bread. Until a few hundred years ago, in the region of Aix and in the Alps near Italy, ruins were still to be found of monuments raised to the glory of Roman bakers. Having a good baker in one's retinue—like having one in your neighborhood today—was a reason for contentment. In Paris, there are streets that bear the names of medieval bakers, such as the Rue Tiquetonne, though nothing is remembered of the baker who traded there other than his stout Breton name.

In the villages, *seigneurs* controlled the economy of bread, but in the towns and cities of the Middle Ages, independent bakers thrived. They were known as *talemeliers,* after the sticks on which they tallied their accounts. By 1300 in Paris, there were 131 *talemeliers* and five female *talemelières,* under the jurisdiction of the *grand panetier,* the royal baker. One of his duties was to collect the *plancheoirs,* the slabs of bread that served as plates during royal banquets, soaking up the juices of the meats, and distribute them to the poor. He also saw to it that apprentice *talemeliers* served the requisite nine years and paid the hefty tithes to become bakers. They started at the age of fourteen, like Roland and his father, and had to be of legitimate birth, well mannered, loyal to the king, and free of communicable or dangerous illnesses.

Until the end of the Middle Ages, monks such as the Capetians oversaw the spiritual and technical qualities of bread. The *boulanger,* as he was now called, was also considered a sorcerer: With water, ground seed, and fire, he created bread, the staff of life. The flames of his oven were associated with those of the devil, who was often nicknamed *le boulanger.* To protect himself, the pious baker paid homage to a saint. Of great importance was the cult of Saint Lazarus, for his protection against leprosy. *Boulangers* feared that the heat of their ovens provoked this disease. In the heart of old Paris was a hospital that took in the leprous, with a chapel endowed by a *confrérie* of *boulangers*. The *confréries*, or brotherhoods, of bakers were secretive—like that other body of medieval artisans, the masons—and powerful: Stained-glass windows in the important Gothic cathedral at Chartres showing bakers at work in a *fournil* were endowed in the thirteenth century by brotherhoods of *boulangers*, who by then had also acquired from the crown the status of a *corporation*, or guild.

The official patron saint of bakers, however, is Saint Honoré, who was born in the sixth century to a wealthy family in Picardie. One day, as his nurse was baking at the oven, the boy was suddenly bathed in celestial rays, and a divine oil of annunciation appeared on his forehead. The nurse refused to believe these signs, and her bread cart was transformed into a plum tree. Honoré later became the bishop of Amiens, a city north of Paris surrounded by wheat fields. He made many conversions to the new Christian faith in a region where the pagan Goddess of the Corn was still a powerful deity. It was against this spirit of the fields that Saint Honoré had to prove his abilities. In 1060, during a terrible drought, his episcopal chair was carried into the fields and abundant rains fell. Under Louis XIV the same thing was tried again, this time to stop rains that were drowning the crops. By then, Saint Honoré had been adopted as the patron saint of *boulangers*, who paraded his relics once a year, giving out bread to all.

These relics were brought to Paris and kept in the church of Saint Honoré, founded in 1204 on the Rue Saint Honoré, where they remained until the Revolution. In disgust at the incapacity of *boulangers* to nourish them, a mob sacked the church and the icons vanished.

Just a decade before, in 1778, Parmentier had published the *Parfait boulanger*. A member of the Academy of Science of Lyon and the *Collège de Pharmacie* in Paris, he would have scoffed at such superstition and attributed to nature the record number of lean years in the eighteenth century. To alleviate the repeated famines after poor wheat crops, he promoted the potato in France, lending his name to *hachis Parmentier,* French shepherd's pie. In the *Parfait boulanger,* he blamed the misery of famine on mismanagement, and to see what could be done, he set out to follow wheat "from the moment it's in the hands of man until it's transformed into bread." As a guide, he enlisted a certain *maître* Brocq, baker at the Ecole Militaire des Invalides.

Parmentier considered bakers to be both artisans and shopkeepers. To win them over to his methods, he rhapsodized the poor *boulanger:* "They work in a noisy atmosphere, wreathed in dust and smoke from their fires, at the hour when nature is at rest. They can only give in to sleep when the rest of us are at play. Yet often, after all they give us, they end up beggars or infirm, among the criminal and the lazy." He mentioned the strict regulations that bound them and paid tribute to the generosity of bakers in Burgundy, who had given away bread in a recent famine. With greater numbers of people living in towns, *boulangers,* he noted, bore the brunt of anger at bread shortages.

Parmentier began by marveling at the 360 varieties of wheat then in existence, but bewailing the fact that "we have known for some time the natural history of the snake-eating secretary bird of Virginia, the mountains of Peru and the roots of Brazilwood trees, but we don't know that of wheat." Opinion was divided in his day. "Some authors say that in Sicily—an isle once the most fertile in wheat in the world— there is a terrain that has long produced a grass like our wheat. Those who deny the existence of wild wheat pretend it is a grass that nature has lost to history." He cited de Bouffon, who was of the view that wheat being the plant man worked the most, "it has changed to the point of no longer existing in nature." To this day, the wheat we eat—*Triticum vulgare*—has never been found growing wild. Its ancestors are now thought to be varieties known in Europe as einkorn and emmer, whose ears have fewer grains, that grew wild in the eastern Mediterranean between Syria and Iraq. It's still not known who created it, perhaps as long as seven thousand years ago. The wheat of the pharaohs, which was very much like ours, was already the product of careful cross-breeding. Parmentier insisted on continuous selection as the key to a good crop. He damned superstitions about corn blight and rubigo. "A favorable season produces a robust wheat." As evidence, he cited examples of wheat kept for decades, and related how, in 1744, the royal family ate bread made with wheat that had been preserved in the citadel of Metz for two centuries.

From the grain, he passed to milling, recommending the proper upkeep of mills often becalmed by droughts, floods, and frosts, or by poor construction, that "languish, suspending milling and increasing the price of flour." When it came to making dough, he discouraged the use of too much *levure artificiel,* or brewer's yeast. "Kneading is harder," he admitted, "but the bread is more balanced and tastier. Water, without which the yeast or leaven would act only weakly on the flour, is not of the consequence we pretend. It's the temperature of the water and the quantity that matter." Kneading is crucial. "The strength, the firmness, the whiteness and evenness of the crumb are indications of the care taken." As for rising: "When it's too risen, bread is flat and bitter. That's why you see the *boulanger* so agitated when it comes to judging the degree of fermentation, and stopping it by the violent means of cooking." He discouraged adding salt. "One always abuses the best things. Happily most don't use it because of the expense. The fruity taste of *noisette* that milling, kneading, rising and cooking develop in bread is masked and destroyed by the bitterness of salt."

Parmentier praised the baker's mastery of the oven, his instinct for temperature, and the placing of loaves in the oven that "even usage doesn't bestow on all bakers." Finally, he advocated buying bread from the *boulanger,* rather than baking it oneself. "It's cumbersome, with a mediocre result. Religious houses—always so careful of health and economy—have given it up. In most large towns, people no longer make their bread at home. Even in the new towns, people who still cull their grains prefer to sell them."

A trainee *boulanger* preparing croissants at the École de Boulangerie de Paris,
the first-ever school for bakers in France, founded in 1929 by the Grands Moulins de Paris,
suppliers of flour.

The *boulanger* made his way from the village to the city; but the *pâtissier* came from the kitchens of a royal palace. Bread is of the people, but *pâtisserie* is of the nobility. *"Qu'ils mangent de la brioche!"* Marie-Antoinette is said to have scoffed when her husband Louis XVI was warned that the people had no bread. Less than a century later, they were doing just that. The privilege of consuming *pâtisserie fine* was no longer exclusive to the aristocracy.

Looking for ways to increase their revenue, *boulangers* began baking *viennoiserie* at the end of the nineteenth century, aided by the newly available and easy-to-use dried yeast sold by Baron Springer. Anything that was light and delicate as a waltz came from Vienna. The fashion for *viennoiserie* was launched by a bakery on the Rue de Richelieu owned by the Prussian officer Zang, which sold cakes made with fine white flour, milk, sugar, and brewer's yeast. The term is used nowadays to describe the cakes most commonly baked by *boulangers*. It encompasses *pain au lait* made with milk and *pain au raisin* made with milk, raisins, and some egg custard, as well as brioches made with butter, and croissants and *pain chocolat* made with flaky pastry. Croissants made with flaky pastry are a French invention. Until the First World War, they were made in what was called the Prussian style, and were simply crescent-shaped *pain au lait*. (Ironically, it was the aforementioned Austrian princess Marie-Antoinette who launched the vogue for croissants.) The first baker to sell croissants in Paris was on the Rue Dauphine. In the 1930s, there was still a sign outside his premises that proclaimed "the best croissants," but this, and the bakery, have gone. The best cakes, as we shall see, are always ephemeral.

The *boulanger* and the *pâtissier* belong to different professions, and practice different arts. But it's common to see *Boulangerie-Pâtisserie* above bakery premises. In addition to selling *viennoiserie*, by associating with a *pâtissier* or by earning a *brevet élémentaire* in cake making themselves, *boulangers* can sell more sophisticated cakes. Many *boulangers* nowadays are also *pâtissiers*. The *boulanger* provides a staple; the products of the *pâtissier* are luxuries. But they're an indulgence few would dispense with. Aside from circuses, perhaps, Parisians love nothing more than cakes and pastries. During the week there is the office worker's morning croissant, and the schoolchild's tea-time *pain au raisin* or *pain chocolat*. On Sundays the windows of bakeries like Béchu are full of lavish *gâteaux,* all of which are sold by lunchtime, to be devoured the same afternoon.

Boulangers are respected, but *pâtissiers* become famous. A baker is a necessity: Without a good baker, the village isn't a village. But without a good *pâtisserie,* the town isn't a town. *Pâtisseries* are known as *maisons,* suggestive of their status, while *boulangeries* are called *affaires,* indicative of their turnover. *Boulangeries* are constrained by the humble associations of bread. Even in modern cities, the *boulangerie* is the center of a neighborhood. It is reassuring, even a bit shabby, because the baker is so busy, so preoccupied with his bread. The smell of a *boulangerie* is a warm reminder that hunger will soon be sated. Regrettably, the smell of a *pâtisserie* is nowadays rather anodyne. There is no waft of warm sugar and wheat baking, just a faint chill from the air conditioning.

*P*âtisserie is first of all an art, not a commerce. A true, noble *pâtisserie* is a large, fancy emporium that doesn't sell bread, other than some Viennese loaves. It is consecrated to the making of pastries and cakes. The ones on the boulevards of Paris and other big cities are veritable temples, full of dainty parcels of luxury and frivolity.

The style of decor in these *pâtisseries* has changed along with the styles of *gâteaux*. Behind glass doors that slide silently open as you approach them, very little remains of the Second Empire, the period when *pâtisseries* began to flourish. The ornate plaster moldings on the ceilings and cornices have long gone, replaced by smooth, shining surfaces. The chandeliers have been removed to make way for halogen lighting. The painted wall panels, with their themes of elysian splendor and cherubic delight, have been superseded by an idea of elegance inherited from Art Deco. Lines are straight; tones are full, rich, and even. The color schemes are often brown and cream, suggestive of the two essential flavorings, chocolate and vanilla. French blue is popular, too, recalling the aristocratic origins of *pâtisserie*.

Lavish, ostentatious cake decoration went out with heavy drapes. *Gâteaux* now have a discreet charm, plain on the outside apart from a signature and a crystallized leaf, but inside there are flavors poised for a fatal battle: chocolate and mint, raspberry and chocolate. Fruits are still decorative, however, being fashionably natural. The colorful fruit compositions have a neat perfection under their glaze of *apricotine*. (If it's possible to improve on a strawberry, *pâtissiers* can do it.) Where once everything was a cream, now everything is a mousse, for elegance above all must be light and effortless. The murals painted on the wall panels have been covered with mirrors or lacquered as smooth as the chocolate glaze on the opéra cakes in the refrigerated display trays. The salesgirls still wear pinafores tied with bows, however, and are always impatient to serve the customers. And making up your mind remains the most sublime of agonies.

It was a nineteenth-century chef, Carême, who had the idea of fashioning individual portions of large cakes, which he called *pâtisserie de main* because they could be held in the hand. Instead of buying one large *gâteau*, you could buy pieces of several different ones. These are the little cakes laid out in neat rows, each with a nameplate at the front—though there are so many names that one is rapidly lost. One nineteenth-century cookbook gave recipes for three thousand *gâteaux* and *entremets*, delicacies that we would think of now as desserts. Asking what they're made of doesn't help either. The reply is an intoxicating carbohydrate welter, a sugar rush of things soaked in kirsch, filled with mocha cream, and caramelized. But somehow a choice is made. If you buy one cake, it's put inside a paper pyramid, which can be carried only on the palm of the hand, so you can't get very far with it and must consume it soon, which was your intention anyway.

Buy more cakes, or one large *gâteau,* and you are given a box with the name of the *maison* and the mention that it also produces its own sweets, chocolates, and ice creams, bound by a ribbon with a bow to hook the finger through to carry it home.

The French word *pâtisserie* comes from *pistores,* the Roman name for bakers. The Romans didn't distinguish between bakers of bread and bakers of cakes, and neither did the Gauls. But cakes require special techniques. To this day they denote a special, often ceremonial occasion. In the Middle Ages, that meant they were linked to religion. For many centuries, only nuns and monks had the time and expertise to produce cakes and biscuits. The madeleines of which Proust was so fond were probably first made by monks. With the development of towns, some bakers started to specialize in cakes. By the end of the Middle Ages, these bakers had formed into guilds, and in 1440 they successfully petitioned to deny *boulangers* the right to bake cakes.

A description of the wares of a late-medieval French *pâtisserie* comes from the *Pastissier François,* one of the rarest of cookbooks, published in Amsterdam in 1655 by Louis and Daniel Elsevier. The two brothers had already published a successful book about gardening, the *Jardinier François,* and surmised that a manual of French cake making would be profitable, too. The author was a certain François Pierre, known as

La Varenne, master chef to the Marquis d'Uxelles. The *Pastissier François* became rare because it was a manual, handled by generations of sticky-fingered apprentices. The crinkled, yellow pages of surviving copies are covered in brown smudges, traces of butter or milk dried into opaque circles like the age rings of a tree.

La Varenne devotes several chapters to various ways of cooking ham *en croute* or, when they were in season, stag, wild boar, and deer. An eighteenth-century engraving of a *pâtisserie* in Diderot's *Encyclopedie* shows game hanging plentifully from the ceiling and meats being prepared for baking in *tourtes* and *friands,* rolls of meat in puff pastry. Rivalry between *boulangers* and *pâtissiers* sometimes became a triangular conflict with *charcutiers,* who charged that *pâtissiers* selling ham encased or rolled in pastry infringed on their trade, because the ham had already been cooked. To this day, a *pâté en croute* can only be bought from a *charcutier* or *traiteur,* a take-out shop that sells savories.

The distinction between sweet and savory is quite recent, dating from the nineteenth century. The medieval *pâtissier* employed a very different range of flavors for *tourtes* and *pastés.* A *tourte* is a pie with a top crust and a *pasté* is a triangular fold of flaky pastry stuffed with mincemeat. In Britain they're called pasties. Around the shores of the Mediterranean they're known as *pastillas,* from the Roman *paste* meaning pastry. These are some of the oldest delicacies of European cuisine, dating back at least to ancient Greece, and also some of the most exquisite, combining wheat, meat, and the flavors of honey, nuts, and flowers.

The *pastés* described by La Varenne are made with meats like hare and goose and seasoned with *espice douce,* a "sweet spice" that consisted of two parts ginger and one part ground peppercorns, with some grated nutmeg, crushed cinnamon, and cloves. The fever for spices in Europe originated with the knights who brought them back from the Crusades. They also brought back the *beignet,* or doughnut; in Syria, on one of the last Crusades, Saint Louis was given doughnuts flavored with cinnamon. Spices weren't needed to preserve food—

salt would do that—and though they added flavor, their real function was social. A taste for spices was part of the new manners by which an emerging metropolitan elite distanced itself from the peasantry.

A recipe for a *pasté à la cardinale* given by La Varenne calls for a mince of chicken, veal, bone marrow, pine nuts, and raisins from Corinth. "Some people add sugar to this sort of *pasté,*" notes the author. The craving for sugar would soon cure customers of their ability to distinguish between raisins from Corinth and those from Malaga.

The Greek general Niarkos went with Alexander the Great to India in the fourth century B.C. and saw a "reed" that "produced honey without the aid of bees." Use of sugar in India can be traced back five thousand years. In the old Indian language of Sanskrit, the word *śākkara* originally meant sand, and came to describe sugar. This became *sukkar* in Arabic, *sákharon* in Greek, *zucchero* in Italian, *sucre* in French, and sugar in English. With the name came techniques of crystallizing sugar from the residue of crushed and boiled cane, which spread slowly westward. In biblical times, sugar was still rare. There are numerous references to honey in the Gospels but only two to cane sugar.

The Moorish conquests of Spain and southern France in the eighth century left a taste for sugar that was satisfied by Venetian refineries for the next five hundred years. It was this sugar, brought from the East via Egypt to Venice, that sweetened the macaroons and frangipane cream to which Catherine de Medici was so partial. But cane is a tropical plant, and its delicious and stimulating refined product remained an imported luxury. As late as 1736, a quantity of cane sugar was listed along with gems in the dowry of Princess Maria-Theresa of Hungary. Sugar—like cloves, cinnamon, and nutmeg—was still rare and expensive when La Varenne wrote the *Pastissier François*. The biscuits that Catherine de Medici offered guests at the

Only *pâtissiers* would dare to try to improve on a strawberry.
These tarts from Poujauran are available only when strawberries are in season.

court—made of equal volumes of finely sifted white flour, sugar, and crushed almonds imported from Piemonte—would have been beyond the pockets of customers in La Varenne's bakery.

A piece of fruit, perhaps lightly spiced, provided the sweetness for La Varenne's simple fare of *beignets* and *chossons,* or turnovers. They had a glaze achieved by brushing them with beaten eggs. The more yolk, said La Varenne, the more golden the glaze, and he gave a professional tip: *"Pastissiers* put honey in their basting mixes to spare eggs." Honey, like wheat, is one of the earliest cultivated foods. The pastries of antiquity were all sweetened with honey. (In good Greek and Turkish bakeries, they still are.) Honey was the main sweetener available to the medieval *pastissier,* who would have wanted to keep his eggs for *aumelettes,* flans, and the like. La Varenne gives many recipes for egg-based dishes, an important part of the seventeenth-century *pastissier*'s trade.

A certain amount of what would once have been termed sweetness also came from the flour, eggs, and milk or butter themselves, though sugar-heavy diets have largely destroyed our capacity to appreciate this distinction, and the subtle flavors of these foods have been neutralized in the name of hygiene and yield. Conditions used to vary from valley to valley, village to village, and field to field, and so did the taste of the produce. The quality of La Varenne's cakes depended on the land husbandry that produced good grain or milk in a countryside that had yet to be ploughed into endless uniform furrows.

By our standards, the cakes sold in a *pâtisserie* at the time of La Varenne were not very fancy. Tarts made with *fromage blanc* or fresh soft cheese mixed with flour and egg were the ancestors of the quiche. Flans or custard pies were common in the Middle Ages, but the staple of *pâtisserie* was the simple fruit tart. Rabelais in his *Pantagruel* describes sixteen types of *tourtes* and twenty types of tart, and as many varieties of fruit tart as there are fruits; that is still the case today. A domestic standby in French homes—an unpretentious, maternal item of *pâtisserie* that anyone can make—tarts are often the centerpieces in *pâtisseries* and restaurants, especially in autumn when figs and berries are ripe. At that time, it's common to see a dessert table laden only with tarts of different deep, glistening colors: ruby cassis and violet *myrtille* or bilberry; plums of all colors: yellow, red, purple, and the green Reine Claudes.

Often the fruits were set in a *crème pâtissière,* a custard, as was the *pasté de poyres,* a pear tart. At least one of the main types of pastry already existed in the Middle Ages. The *pâte feuilletée*—pastry rolled out and sandwiched with butter so that it will bake in leaves (*feuilles*)—was known to the Romans, who made it by baking the leaves separately. Spreading butter between the layers so they could be baked at the same time was an innovation of the sixteenth century, often attributed to the chefs Catherine de Medici brought with her to France, along with the arts of the Italian Renaissance, when she came to wed Henry II.

Although we could share the medieval enjoyment of fruit tarts made with strawberries, peaches, plums, or apricots, we would be unlikely to relish instantly a *tourte de racines*—literally a root pie. La Varenne suggested using roots of chervis—a slightly acid-tasting grass—cleaned, boiled lightly, and crushed, then mixed with equal amounts of broken white bread and the same amount of *crème pâtissière.* He advised seasoning with a "pinch" of sugar, salt, rosewater, cinammon, and perhaps some pine nuts or raisins and lemon peel. He knew the culinary and commercial value of sugar, but could only afford to use it sparingly. He did, though, frown on another new practice: "Many *pastissiers* now use yeast or the froth of beer instead of putting fresh leaven in their pastry, because it makes the dough rise faster and their merchandise lighter, though it's less good for the health." The issue was considered so vital at the time that Louis XIV set up a committee of six nobles and six doctors to decide on it. As a result, the use of brewer's yeast was forbidden by royal decree, unless it came from a local brewery and was sure to be fresh.

Jean-Luc Poujauran outside his *boulangerie* on the Rue Jean Nicot, Paris.

The *Pastissier François* is full of clear, simple recipes, which are surprisingly familiar in essence despite the centuries. La Varenne made his *crème pâtissière,* for example, by boiling some "good cow's milk" and adding a separate mix of egg and flour. Some salt and butter was all he used for flavor. "Let it simmer and stir it like porridge. It will be cooked in a quarter of an hour; then one pours it into a bowl and you keep this composition, which *pastissiers* call *cresme* and which one uses in many pieces." Indeed, it was this cream, a simple egg custard, that helped the *pâtisserie* of today to coalesce. Its appearance in La Varenne's cookbook is evidence of the skill and care employed even then. The milk must have required careful storage, but by boiling it, La Varenne was subjecting it to a process recommended much later by Louis Pasteur. The milk available then was more unctuous and fatty than the homogenized milk we have. It appears that his customers relished this texture, and expected his creams to be buttery rather than sweet.

His clientele would have been townfolk with sophisticated tastes, compared to those of the villagers who still made up the majority of the French population, and who might occasionally put a loaf with raisins in the communal oven, but for whom a cake usually meant a religious or ceremonial occasion. In the countryside, people were not likely to have been able to afford much sugar and spice. They might have added honey, nuts, or other flavorings to an unleavened dough and left small pats in the oven as it cooled, producing biscuits, from the French *bis* (meaning twice or extra) *cuit* (cooked). Coming to town, they must have marveled at the science of creating an artificial cream.

In the window of Poujauran, a small but celebrated *boulangerie-pâtisserie* in the seventh *arrondissement* of Paris, there is a row of little *tartes aux pignons* made with pine nuts and honey, exactly as they would have been in La Varenne's day. The small, firm, milky blond pine nuts are set upright and packed generously together, rather than laid sparsely on top. Jean-Luc Poujauran is proud of this tart, made with honey, which he prefers to sugar in *pâtisserie*. It's nutritious and balanced, with an unusual, refreshingly nutty flavor. He uses only the best pine nuts from Spain, which cost four times as much as the ones from North Africa or China. "But with those," he sighs, "the taste just isn't the same."

In his bakery are other cakes one might have found in the Middle Ages, like lemon tarts and madeleines. There are also *canelles,* made of a fluffy egg-and-flour concoction like a pancake mix, cooked in hot copper cups and caramelized on top. They are a speciality of a baker in Bordeaux, near the town where Jean-Luc was raised. But it isn't a good day for the *canelles,* which are sensitive to the weather. They're soft, and that usually means it's going to rain.

In his *laboratoire,* Jean-Luc is trying to concoct a pistachio macaroon. Not that this master baker in his late thirties—who is also a *pâtissier, chocolatier,* and *glacier,* and supplies bread to eighty establishments in Paris, including the prestigious Tour d'Argent restaurant and the Hotel Crillon—is having difficulty experimenting with macaroons. They have been baked and eaten in France since the Renaissance. Before he opened his own bakery, Jean-Luc worked for a year with Ladurée in his shop on the Rue Royale; Ladurée makes the best macaroons in Paris and sells nothing but macaroons all day long—expensive, irresistible macaroons. But from the old, Jean-Luc is looking for something new.

The decor of his *boutique,* for instance, is a tasteful *Belle Époque,* recreated from pieces he found in bakeries built during the rosy decades before the First World War. The general prosperity of those years meant that even modest bakers could refurbish, removing medieval iron grilles and installing hand-painted glass panels like the ones Poujauran rescued. He would be delighted to see his bakery classified as a historical building, as are some old *boulangeries:* "That way, when I'm dead it would stay the same." (For many *boulangers,* finding their premises on the Ministry of Culture's list is a nightmare, as it means they can't renovate except, at high cost, in exactly the same style. It's not uncommon for an owner to learn that his bakery has been listed the day after it has been stripped for modernization, and in this way many have disappeared.)

The only modern item in Poujauran's *boutique* is the video lens mounted in the corner, allowing him to observe the reactions of customers from his office. The other new tool is the fax, on which recipes flurry back and forth in the middle of night.

The problem of the pistachio macaroon is just a distraction. He has been trying for the last two months to come up with a new recipe for a madeleine, a small sponge cake that has been baked and eaten in France for even longer than the macaroon.

"Do you know how many recipes there are already for madeleines?" he asks. "Eighteen."

Each is good, each a little different. Jean-Luc Poujauran is intent on creating a nineteenth.

The problem, as always, is ingredients. For a good macaroon, for example, "You must start with the best pistachios. Then you must cook them exactly right, so they don't lose too much of their oil. You mustn't use vanilla, because you want them to taste of pistachio, after all, with just a hint of hazelnut." Then there is the problem of almonds. It was the almonds that Catherine de Medici loved in a macaroon. Italian girls have always had a weakness for almonds, especially almonds smoothly coated with sugar tinted in delicate pastels. Sugared almonds are given away in little packets at weddings and christenings. Sucking them summarizes the deepest happiness. But the almonds Jean-Luc is using are not from Piemonte. "The best almonds now come from California," he says, nodding in affirmation as though this might be hard to believe. "They've made great progress over there," he acknowledges. The macaroon he is preparing will be nothing less than perfect. But still he isn't satisfied. It's going to cost too much. He wants it to cost less, without sacrificing quality.

Jean-Luc Poujauran began his professional career in the 1970s, when nostalgia for nonindustrial foods was first budding. He had started baking long before that, at his father's side in the *fournil* of the family bakery in Mont de Marsan, in southwest France. "I had grown up with bread," he explains, "so I decided to do different breads."

But artisanal skills demand appropriate materials. He had to search for stone-ground flour, impossible to find at that time. A thousand years of progress in milling in the Paris region had done away with both the natural and the picturesque. The windmills of Montmartre had been replaced by huge roller mills housed in what seem like tall, ramshackle *châteaux,* architectural curiosities situated on the Seine at the Tolbiac bridge and in the suburb of Saint Denis. The charm of the white sails had been replaced by a constant thunder from the metal rollers that ground and tore the grain day and night, pouring out good quality but uniform white wheat flour for the millions of baguettes eaten every day.

When the wheat grain is ground by stone and bolted, or sifted, with care, its texture is preserved, resulting in better flavor. Customers make special trips to buy loaves made with such wheat from Poujauran. The ecology movement has made many converts in France, as much for gastronomic as ideological reasons. Naturally grown, untreated, and lightly processed foods taste better. Jean-Luc Poujauran knows about authentic techniques and traditional ingredients, but he has brought urban sophistication and a great personal finesse to their use.

His tastes aren't rustic, however. He prefers a sourdough bread that isn't too sour, for instance, "so you can eat it with something." Most sourdough loaves are made with brewer's yeast, or with a leaven that is started with yeast. On the shelves of Poujauran is a loaf made with *levain naturel.* The raising agent for this

Bread from Jean-Luc Poujauran's small *boulangerie-pâtisserie*
is delivered to some of the best restaurants in Paris.

loaf is a *chef,* a piece of stale sourdough that he began cultivating seventeen years ago. "I learned how to make it from my father," he says. Sometimes he helps out bakers who have gone away and left the refrigerator thermostat too high—killing their *chef*—by giving them a chunk of his own.

When he went to Korea to test recipes for an Asian bakery chain, Jean-Luc took some of his seventeen-year-old *chef* with him in a colander wrapped in linen. It survived the long plane ride. His cakes came out light and tasty and the loaves were chubby as babies.

The *chef,* or *mère,* meaning mother, as it's also called, is at the heart of the alchemy of bread. Without leaven, bread would be flat, dense, and hard to digest.

Jean-Luc Poujauran's *chef* is a football-size ball of dough, of a creamy gray color, with a slight smell of ethanol. Whenever he takes a piece to bake a batch of loaves, he adds more flour and water. So it's not really seventeen years old, even though the process of rotting actually began earlier—with a piece of his father's *chef.*

It takes patience to create a good leaven. Like grape juice that becomes wine, the dough must ferment in the right conditions. The tiny mushrooms that grow as the wheat rots, feeding on sugars in the grain, are sensitive to temperature and humidity. Some of these microscopic spores are already present in the wheat and some come from the atmosphere, resulting in subtle differences in the character of the bread from one bakery to the next. Brewer's yeast is simply one highly active spore present in wheat, named *Saccharomyces cerevisiae,* that's isolated and fed on molasses left over from making beer. Because it has risen with only one busy spore, bread made with brewer's yeast—though it rises more easily and has a lighter consistency—has a less complex taste.

The French tradition in baking is to use a natural leaven. In some coastal regions of Normandy, shellfish called *manço* were used for leaven; they were crushed and placed in a sack with the dough. Sea water, too, was used for baking in some places, and in the Middle Ages people living on the coast were envied their salty bread.

French settlers introduced the painstaking techniques of baking with leaven to San Francisco in the nineteenth century, where the bread they baked came to be known as sourdough. Nowadays, for convenience, this sort of bread is often not made with what Jean-Luc Poujauran calls a natural leaven—one that was started with only flour and water—but with a leaven that was started with brewer's yeast. For their *pains au levain,* many bakers in France also use a leaven started with brewer's yeast. The result is bread with a less interesting character, less rich in taste and sometimes sour to the point of being acid.

Having created a range of loaves that sit on the white tablecloths of the best restaurants in Paris, Jean-Luc has turned to cakes. He is interested in simple cakes because he thinks they're better suited to a *boulangerie,* which his bakery primarily is, and because "you can keep prices down." Elaborate decoration, he says, "is not me." He wants to create cakes that aren't too heavy in sugar or fat "because people come back." They're to be made with only the freshest ingredients. He uses only fresh fruits, for example. "That's why there isn't much in the window today," he apologizes proudly. He enthuses about *palmiers* he baked the day before, all of which are gone. "They were crusty, sweet, and fresh. They shouldn't be eight days old; they should be eight hours old!"

His father didn't bake *pâtisserie,* just apple tarts on Sunday, croissants, *pain chocolat,* apple turnovers, and a pastry called a *jesuit,* shaped like the triangular hats of the priests. "It was his speciality, and people came from far away for it: just *pâte feuilletée* with a layer of almond cream and another layer of *crème pâtissière*, cut into triangles."

Jean-Luc confesses that when he came to Paris, he peered in the window of the grandiose *pâtisserie* where he was due to start his apprenticeship and his heart sank. "I was frightened," he says. The profusion and richness of all the cakes made him nauseous. The decorative perfection left him cold.

It was arranged that he would work in the sixteenth *arrondissement* under a *pâtissier* named Gervais, who, when he retired at sixty-five, began to work gratis for someone else because he had what Jean-Luc calls, with a hint of woe, *"le virus du métier"* ["the virus of the profession"]. From Gervais he learned how the fancy *gâteaux* were made. Gervais had been a competitor of Gaston Lenôtre, whose *boutique* was in the same neighborhood. Lenôtre now has a factory outside Paris, supplying luxury *gâteaux* in frozen perfection, what Jean-Luc calls "going industrial."

Though he delves into the past for recipes, going industrial is what interests Jean-Luc. "People are going back to tradition. I'd like to adapt artisanal recipes for the supermarket: using medieval recipes but not medieval production methods. I want people to be able to share it. If you can get the same quality with mass production, why not?"

His small shop serves as the basis for his marketing studies. Of his more than one thousand customers a day, many come from afar, especially for his *galette des rois* in January—one of the best in Paris—made with "fresh almonds and butter that hasn't been in the fridge for six months." There is no secret. It comes down to the quality of the ingredients and the work involved. Jean-Luc employs three *pâtissiers* and five *boulangers,* one of whom interrupts us to tell him that the *chambre de pousse,* the refrigerator where the dough is left to rise, urgently needs his attention. Jean-Luc pays no mind.

"I worked for six years at different *maisons* in Paris but at each, I only found one or two things I liked. Of the thirty-two cakes we do here, only two have chocolate, for instance. Chocolate is something different. It doesn't agree with the dust from the flour. It should be elsewhere." He doesn't bake meringues, either, although it's a handy way to dispose of surplus egg whites and make use of the fading heat of the oven. And he also doesn't like choux pastries. The first recipe for fluffy choux, which means cabbage, was given by Carême in 1815. It was one of the aristocratic delights first made accessible by that great chef. For Jean-Luc, however, choux pastry is "too fatty." In fact, he confesses he doesn't like anything that came after Carême.

It might seem that he has a purist view of *pâtisserie;* and there is something ascetic about the wares in his shop. So wholesome are the cakes and loaves that they look as though they were prepared by monks. But then again, there is nothing more divine than a pistachio macaroon.

Jean-Luc has simply been applying to *pâtisserie* the precepts of the culinary and dietary changes of the last few decades. He uses fresh ingredients, prepared in ways that preserve their natural flavors. He obviously has the *virus du métier* himself. Like all great *pâtissiers,* he is obsessed with *pâtisserie*, a science anyone can learn but an art few can master, whose precepts he wants to renew.

"Sugar is a drug; chocolate is a drug. Instead of lunch, a secretary buys a chocolate bar from the supermarket and eats that and then has a coffee. She's in a nervous state all afternoon. I see them. It's not a good, balanced diet." He wants to see his customers return, but he doesn't want them to be unable to get through the door. "I'm convinced you can unhook people from those sugary tastes, convinced! *Pâtisserie* has become too sophisticated."

The fastidious Italians thought it indecorous for diners to hold a joint of meat by hand as they carved their slice, so they used new devices called forks. Their culinary arts—partly the fruit of long contact via Venice with the Orient—were to be much copied in France, thanks to the fourteen-year-old Florentine bride of Henry II. To present their son to the nation, Catherine de Medici went on tour in 1564 with the court, which was at that time bigger than many towns. In addition to artists, decorators, engineers, astronomers, jesters, and physicians, she took her chefs and *pâtissiers* to delight and impress. For two years they shared their skills in the kitchens of noble houses and modest inns. Though it was done purely for political reasons, everyone was given a taste of her Italian refinement.

She served her guests sorbets—such was Italian food technology that it could produce ice in midsummer— and she is often said to have introduced the French to brioches, petit fours, and éclairs. In fact, the brioche, whose quality depended on butter, was a peasant cake from the northern, dairy-farming parts of France. The petit four could have been invented by any royal *pâtissier* with the time and inspiration to make smaller versions of existing *entremets;* some say it was by Carême, two centuries later. And the choux pastry for the éclair is sometimes attributed to Fauvel, a predecessor of Carême, who named his choux buns *saint-honorés,* after the patron saint of bakers. Catherine did, however, popularize the macaroon, made with almonds, sugar, and egg whites. Almonds at that time were a great delicacy. Hazelnuts, walnuts, and especially chestnuts— plentiful and easily stored—were basic foodstuffs, but almonds were not native to France. They were reputed to be an aphrodisiac, perhaps since they came—like all things seductive—from Italy.

A century after Catherine undertook the improvement of French cuisine and manners, another Italian, Procopio dei Coltelli, opened what was to be the forerunner of the *salon de thé,* or tearoom. Most cafés of the time were little more than stalls in the street, and he wanted to create an upmarket setting in which to sell such Italian delicacies as iced cheeses. He filled his premises with mirrors, chandeliers, glass, and silverware, all of which offered a dazzling refinement to the wives of *nouveau riche* merchants and lawyers when he opened in 1686. The demand for his confectionery, preserves, perfumes, and cakes—hitherto reserved for aristocratic families with the staff to prepare them—was fervent.

Procope's, as it was known, is now a restaurant. But his idea was much copied, most successfully during the Belle Époque by Angelina's on the Rue de Rivoli, where wives continue to spend their afternoons agonizing over the damage of a *divorce*—in this case calorific, as it's the name of an éclair—before succumbing anew. A high, sculpted ceiling—ornate plaster moldings known in France as *pâtisserie*—gives one the uncanny sense of actually being inside a huge *gâteau*. The vast salon bustles with a unique kind of agitation: the sashaying of the waitresses, clad in black dresses and white aprons, between tables and serving trolleys laden with gorgeous *pâtisseries;* the plush chairs gliding in and out under plush *derrières;* and the dainty serving of the cakes, followed by a shameless attack that soon gives way to sated indifference at the half-eaten mess that remains.

The most popular drink at Angelina's—just as it was at Procope's—is hot chocolate, made with three parts milk and one part water. The tablets of chocolate are melted in the water first. Tablets are best, not the powdered cocoa resulting from the process invented by Van Houten in 1820, which contains less of the nourishing and stimulating oil.

Chocolate—as a drink, made into confectionery, or added to cakes—is considered a vice of women, a sensual pleasure, like pastries, and especially pastries incorporating chocolate and cream. The bitter taste of chocolate comes from an alkaloid called theobromine, which means food of the gods. It has a less strident effect on the nervous system than the caffeine in coffee, considered a masculine beverage. Drinkers of chocolate were depicted in rococo art as half reclining, often in bed, and for many centuries chocolate was reputed to be an aphrodisiac, the preferred morning drink of women with an idle, leisurely day ahead, like the women who gather in Angelina's. Chocolate cakes, whether simple éclairs or refined opéra cakes with their glass-smooth dark glaze, are the most sinful of all cakes. Nonetheless, chocolate was especially popular with women who belonged to religious orders, nuns with much expertise in baking, which they took with them to the missions in the Americas where chocolate was discovered. The nuns of Lima were famed in the sixteenth century for their chocolate confections. Adding to its appeal was the fact that it could be made into a liquid, and drinks are not proscribed during Lent. For this reason, chocolate first became a popular drink in Catholic countries, the most ardent of which was Spain.

It's to the Aztecs that we owe the pleasure of chocolate. They offered blocks of a dark brown substance to their gods, and the Spanish *conquistadores* noticed that some nobles had the privilege of eating it. This was *xocoatl,* chocolate: the seeds of the cacao tree dried and milled like corn, then mixed with water. The Spaniards tried it mixed with pepper, and they ate chicken cooked in chocolate sauce the way the Aztecs suggested, but weren't immediately won over. It wasn't until cane sugar was added by Portuguese merchants in the Canary Islands, who wanted to get it out of their stores, that the Aztec novelty became a success in Europe. In 1615, the marriage of the Hapsburg princess Anne of Austria to Louis XIII occasioned the introduction of chocolate to France. Anne, only fourteen years old, was addicted to chocolate, a pleasure she had learned during her upbringing in Madrid, and which she was soon sharing with her fourteen-year-old husband and the entire French court. It wasn't long before the French people were clamoring for it, too.

Chocolate—once a little sugar is added—is the most bittersweet, the most melancholy of all gourmandises. Brillat-Savarin, author of *The Physiology of Taste,* wrote of the *mal* of chocolate. He categorized it as the pleasure of the afflicted: "Those who have been too long at their labors, who have drunk too long at the cup of voluptuousness, who feel they have become temporarily inhuman, who are tormented by their families, who find life sad and love ephemeral; they should all eat chocolate and they will be comforted."

By the mid-nineteenth century, when Brillat-Savarin wrote those lines, chocolate had taken a soothing toll on sentiment. Sugar was snowing like angelic bounty on what must have seemed a hitherto sour, dour world.

On his second voyage, Columbus brought sugarcane to the New World. It became one of the principal crops of the European colonies, but supplies of this potent, delicious stimulant were still insufficient to satisfy demand in the Old World. It was the availability of sugar from a crop that could be grown in Europe that allowed chefs like Carême to create what we now think of as *pâtisserie*. German chemists had found that some varieties of beet roots contained large amounts of sugar. At his factory at Passy, then in the suburbs of Paris, Benjamin Delessert succeeded in 1810 in extracting from beets sufficient quantities of this crystal silver to be awarded the *Croix de la Légion d'honneur* by Napoleon. He had opened the doors on a fairytale world, a realm of sugary folly where everything glistened and dissolved on the tongue in a sweet sparkle. France now produces for its own consumption some 2.5 million metric tons of beet sugar per year, and the molasses left over from making beet sugar is used to feed the spores that become brewer's yeast, which in turn raises the cakes made with flour and sugar.

There is one other fundamental flavor in modern *pâtisserie,* and this we also owe to the Aztecs, who used it to improve the taste of *xocoatl.* Cortes was given a drink flavored with it at the court of Montezuma. The Spaniards called it *vainilla,* the diminutive of *vaina,* which means pod, after the bean pods of the tropical

Duchesne, on the Rue Saint Dominique, Paris. A superior old *pâtisserie*.

orchid that yield this sweet, creamy essence. Native to Central America and the Caribbean, the plant is a climber, with aerial roots and flowers that open a few at a time and last for only a day. The beans from the large pods are harvested unripe and have no aroma. Ten days of sweating by night and drying in the sun by day turns them brown. They are then cured for six months, which is when crystals of vanillin develop. Extracted with alcohol and water, this vanillin is what imparts the flavor to ice cream, confectionery, and *pâtisserie*. Until it was synthesized using extracts of oil of cloves, vanilla essence was always in short supply. Perfumers made much use of the intensely sweet aroma, and to procure stocks for themselves they spread a rumor during the nineteenth century that the plant was poisonous. But this caused only a momentary pause in what had become a taste revolution.

Before the introduction of vanilla and chocolate, the essences used in *pâtisserie* were extracted from European plants like anise, *Pimpinella anisum,* which grows in the Loire valley and the Angers region of France, and in Italy and Germany. The seeds from the star-shaped flowers have a cool licoricelike flavor, but little sweetness. *Gimblettes* from the town of Albi in Provence, famed since the thirteenth century, are still made with the local anise, which is greener and has a stronger flavor than the anise of the Loire. (*Gimblettes* are a kind of *échaudé,* a bun boiled or soaked in water or milk to be cooked the following day.) There were various kinds of nuts and dried fruit like raisins and, of course, honey was plentiful in Europe. But the essential flavor of *pâtisserie* was *fleur d'oranger,* orange blossom water, what we would be more likely to think of now as a perfume, like rosewater, which was also used in cookery.

By the nineteenth century, preferences had changed irrevocably. According to Pierre Lacam, a *pâtissier* writing at the time, "The *grandes maisons* hardly use any orange blossom water nowadays, because they put vanilla everywhere, and their cakes have more flavor." Orange blossom was disdained as the flavoring of the *"petit pâtissier,"* who reserved costly vanilla for the cream for his éclairs, and sometimes not even that.

Lacam recalled working in a *maison* where the master *pâtissier* made everything with *fleur d'oranger,* even the *saint-honorés:* "I tried to talk to him about it and I was nearly sacked. But they never sold two *saint-honorés* to the same person."

The availability of new and seductive flavorings, a greater use of butter, better quality flour produced through new milling processes, and the spread of precise cooking techniques heightened the quality of *pâtisserie.* Protective of their thriving commerce, the guild of *pâtissiers* obtained in 1718 the interdiction of the use of butter, eggs, and sugar by anyone outside of the profession. Boulangers were permitted to continue baking only *gâteaux des rois*—large, round *feuilletées* filled with almond cream like a frangipane—since they gave these away to their customers at Epiphany.

"The eighteenth century was the century of the gourmand," wrote Albert Chevallier, *officier de bouche,* or personal chef, to the Prince of Arenberg. "Paris was full of temples raised to *gourmandise:* taverns, cabarets, and all sorts of *pâtisseries,* from the artisanal to the master." According to him, a good half of the street cries struck this chord: *"Échaudés, gâteaux, pastez chaud! A ma brioche, châtands!"*

The *maison* of Bailly, on the Rue Vivienne that leads north out of the Palais Royal, was the first noteworthy *pâtisserie* in Paris. It was in the heart of the theater district, near the Théâtre des Italiens. Whenever the fate of France was in the balance, at moments of greatest upheaval, the Parisians traditionally flocked to hear the arias of La Joconde. They derived further consolation from the *pâtisseries* of Bailly. Nearby was the Théâtre des Variétés, the rendezvous of dissident journalists and politicians during the Revolutionary years, where, according to the critic Merle, "Anything was pretext for mirth and pleasure, everything a spectacle, all the way to the gallery; the *place d'honneur* of the prettiest *habituées."* And after, there was the café Chéron, the restaurant run by Madame Camus, and the *maison* of Bailly, whose wares were lit in the evenings by flickering oil lamps.

One of the apprentices who worked in this illustrious bakery was Marie-Antonin Carême. He was already an accomplished cook, and wanted to master the reputedly more difficult art of pastry cooking. It was there that he learned the techniques he would later set down in *Le Pâtissier Royal.* Carême banished spices from *pâtisserie.* He perfected traditions inherited from the chefs of Catherine de Medici via the likes of Vatel, the famous *maître d'hôtel* who killed himself during a dinner given by the Duc de Condé for the king. It is said that Vatel thought his honor compromised when the fish course failed to arrive from the coast in time, although *pâtissiers* insist he wouldn't have blamed himself for this predicament, and that the real reason for his humiliation was the failure of his first try at an English novelty, plum pudding.

A deprived childhood had left Carême with habits of frugality. He ate little and hardly drank, except for an occasional glass of champagne. He was a man of precision and care—the essential attributes of a pastry chef—with a thin, fine-boned face and narrow shoulders, the marks, ironically, of early malnutrition. His creations were evanescent, as all *pâtisserie* should be. But they have endured through his books. He recorded recipes for madeleines, *génoises, petit pains* (rolls), and choux pastries, as well as for wafers, nougats, tarts, soufflés, meringues, macaroons, and preserves. His painstaking descriptions helped to spread the skills of the French *pâtissier,* and many of his recipes have become standards.

Carême was born in 1784 in the narrow alleyways behind the Rue du Bac, one of twenty-five children, according to Alexandre Dumas in his *Dictionary of Cuisine.* Carême's parents lived in great misery, and his father, who worked as a laborer, was often drunk. One day he took Marie-Antonin for a walk in the fields, returning via the Barrière du Maine, where they stopped at an inn. The father began to speak of his son's future: "Go, *petit,* go out into the world. Find a trade and leave us, for misery is our lot. These are fortunate times and it's enough to have spirit to make yours; go with what God has given you." Carême later recalled the pathetic figure of his father abandoning him there in the street. He never saw his parents again, nor his brothers and sisters. He asked if he could sleep in the tavern and, the following day, they took him on as a kitchen boy to wash, peel, and scrape—this same Carême who would become the *officier de bouche* to the Tsar of Russia and England's George IV.

In 1800 at age sixteen, he left the inn to work in a restaurant. Alert and eager to learn, he left the restaurant to work for Bailly, and then took his skills to the kitchen of Talleyrand, the foreign minister whose table was the most celebrated of the Empire, imitated by all the parvenus of the Revolutionary years. Talleyrand's head chef was the famous Laguepière, whom Carême acknowledged as his master. Laguepière later became the *officier de bouche* to Napoleon, and such was his devotion that he accompanied Napoleon to Russia, preparing fresh bread every day, until he froze to death in the carriage behind the emperor's during the retreat from Moscow. Another great cook, Avice, also worked in Talleyrand's kitchen. It was Avice who gave Carême the inspiration for his life's work, the fabulous *pièces-montées.*

Carême is reputed to have invented the *canapé* and *petit fours*—finger foods of the Restoration—and also the meringue. The mountains of meringues in the windows of *boulangeries* today—colored strawberry pink, chocolate brown, or vanilla white and best when they're big as a fist—wouldn't exist without his experiments. The childish thrill of biting into sugary air, into an object that collapses instantly into sweet, sticky crumbs around a gooey, albuminous center, would otherwise be unknown.

Carême wasn't trying to invent the meringue, however. He was in search of materials out of which to create his *pièces-montées,* staggering architectural desserts made for imperial banquets. He gave precise accounts of their construction in another book, *Pâtissier Pittoresque,* which now seems a work of pure whimsy, though it's a serious *oeuvre,* filled with perspective drawings of so-called *Grands extraordinaires.* These were gigantic, ornamental—though edible—multitiered cakes, confectioned with as much care and detail as the dresses of the empress. Whenever he had a spare moment, Carême, who had taught himself to read and write and had by then entered the service of Bonaparte, hastened to the imperial library to consult designs and drawings. "The main branch of architecture," he insisted, "is confectionery."

Carême was a perfectionist, devoted to detail, and obsessed with verisimilitude. When he was working for Bailly, the new Bourse was under construction in the square opposite, a Doric temple that spurred Carême to wonder how he could bake a Doric cake. In *Pâtissier Pittoresque* he begins by instructing the would-be monumental baker in the differences between Doric, Palladian, and Gothic. He gives plans for cottages, windmills, rocks, ruins, rotundas, pavilions, fountains, waterfalls, vases, castles, cups, baskets, bouquets, shrubs, palms, trophies (marine and military), helmets (antique and modern), lyres, and harps. His materials were sugar, eggs, flour, almonds, and cream. It was easy, he said. It required only "poise, patience, and taste."

Carême even imparted plans for ruins, ruins made of sugar, to which one might well devote one's life. The meringues he invented served as a rocky setting. He mixed flour with gum and powdered marble for his structures and experimented with methods of coloring and forming sugar that became standard for cake decoration. Such cakes are rarely seen nowadays, but once were the centerpieces for lavish banquets. Though it may seem absurd, the secret wish of master *pâtissiers* to this day is to be asked to create one of these assemblies of sugar, flour, and fantasy. They seem to bring out the miniaturist in every pastry chef, the modeler seeking a divine perfection. In the case of a *pâtissier,* this perfection is all the more sublime in that it won't last, but will be devoured, leaving only crumbs, flakes of icing, broken macaroons, and toppled plaster pillars that someone perhaps tried to eat but, to the sorrow of their creator, could not.

By the time Carême published his *Pâtissier Royal* in 1815, the streets north of the Palais Royal were becoming famous for *pâtisserie*. By night, theaters like the Vaudeville roared with a laughing public. By day, clerks of the Banque de France and financiers loitered near the Bourse. Journalists and printers came and went from the offices of the *Charivari* and *Figaro*. And all of their wives came to shop. They bought cakes during the day and *gâteaux* for dinners.

Fashions in cakes changed as fast as fashions in hats. One week they were shaped like stars and comets, the next like pineapples. Inspired by Carême, everyone indulged his and her imagination. Every *maison* had its speciality and everyone had a preference for the wares of a particular *maison*. Liqueurs and creams that gave distinctive flavors were all the rage. Quillet on the Rue de Buci—whose premises are still a *pâtisserie*—originated the *crème Quillet*, a blend of cream, vanilla, butter, barley syrup, and almond essence, sprinkled with ground pistachio nuts. Apprentices who tried to write down the quantities of ingredients that the master threw rapidly, quite by instinct, into the mixing bowl were liable to see their services terminated, a tradition that remains to this day. After Quillet's cream, mocha creams became fashionable, then all manner of creams.

The premises of Bailly, where Carême had worked, were ceded to a certain Félix, who had started by selling brioches from a basket. Félix was famous for the syrup he used to flavor *génoises,* madeleines, and other sponge cakes. Félix himself would prepare it: Once a year when they came into season, he made an infusion of orange blossoms in *eau-de-vie*. After this had fermented, he added kirsch, curaçao, anisette, *eau de noyau* (a spirit made from crushed peach or cherry stones), orange blossom water, and cognac. A dash of this liqueur was enough to flavor a large *gâteau,* but so busy was his trade that a liter would last barely a week.

Félix was one of the largest and busiest *pâtisseries* of its day. As many as thirty-five chefs and apprentices worked in the *laboratoire*. Rollet in the Passage de l'Opéra had twenty-five staff members, and so did Jules Gouffé on the Faubourg St. Honoré who, incidentally, was of the opinion, often expressed by *pâtissiers,* that "A good *pâtissier* can easily become a good chef, but I've never seen a chef become a grand *pâtissier*." Gouffé retired to author several books about cooking, including the *Livre de la Pâtisserie.* Manuals of Parisian cake making were very popular at the time. Louis Bailleux, established right under the Théâtre des Variétés, published in 1856 his *Pâtissier Moderne.* Not greatly literate, he entrusted the writing to two vaudeville authors. The book was full of errors but sold nonetheless.

Towards the end of the nineteenth century, Pierre Lacam published his *Mémorial de la Pâtisserie,* with an astonishing three thousand recipes. Lacam had come to Paris in 1856 to serve an apprenticeship with Félix. He was proud to work in such a celebrated and thriving bakery: "It was a *maison* renowned for its brioches. Nobody has made as many since, nor so well. Every day it was four sacks of flour at midday and four in the evening. Throughout the month of August we made meringues so as not to have to make them in the winter. They were kept in big iron trunks under the oven; four thousand meringues in stock. We supplied all the restaurants and hotels around the Palais Royal. And almond cakes! We ground one hundred kilos of almonds a month for those alone!" Writing in 1891, he already rued the passing of this era and the disappearance of *maisons* like Félix, "or Lançon, with twenty-five employees and such a reputation for the difficult art of decorating cakes with piped icing; or Lannes, for awhile the talk of Paris; and Vincent, with twenty-five employees there too; all of them gone."

The great *maisons* were all grouped around the Palais Royal. Continued Lacam: "There were *pâtissiers* everywhere around this fairytale mansion, but who would know that now? And on the Rue St. Honoré: Girardin with his *nantais,* Finot with his *mathilde,* Barbier, Bourdon, Séjourné and others. Rollet, in the

Passage de l'Opéra, was one of the first in Paris, even more successful than Félix. Gone. The *maison* of Lesserteur on Rue Bourdaloue is sixty years old and has always prospered but what about Bourgeois on the Rue Taitbout? That was a good one, with up to thirty in the *laboratoire*. Closed now. It was the *maison* for *petit fours* stuffed with almond cream. There hasn't been a *maison* in Paris that made more *petit fours*. And the *maison* of Jules Gouffé? Nothing left."

O f the once-glorious nineteenth-century *maisons* there is hardly any trace. But on the Rue Montorgueil that leads from the Louvre up to the villages of Montmartre is a *maison* that still carries the name of the *pâtissier* who founded it long before, in 1734. The location he chose was a short stroll from the Palais Royal, past the fashionable Place des Victoires, near the fruit and vegetable markets of Les Halles. Here Stohrer did what all bakers dream of doing as they survey the miracle in the fire: He made a fortune with a cake.

Ten years ago the premises of Stohrer were running to ruin. A baker named Foissier, who had been there since the Second World War, was keen to retire, but the *quartier* had become dilapidated and no one wanted to take over. The markets of Les Halles had been transferred to the suburbs but gentrification of the area had yet to begin. A large black cat roamed inside the *boutique,* which had been painted dark blue. Discouraged by this somber atmosphere, few people pushed open the creaking door of one of the oldest bakeries in Paris to buy a house specialty that was still halfheartedly concocted in a soot-browned *laboratoire* to the rear.

And so it had been for a number of decades. Nobody seemed to care about the old *pâtisserie* tucked under leaning, crumbling buildings. From time to time, someone would come in, however, to purchase a rum baba and contemplate the painted glass panels, one of which showed an angelic *semeuse* carrying a tray of pastries

The 250-year-old premises on the Rue Montorgeuil, Paris,
where the royal *pâtissier* Stohrer sold the first babas.

in each hand. Wearing a wispy white dress, the sower appears to be pedaling on air, suggesting the lightness of her wares. The painting was done by Paul Baudry, who decorated the foyer of the Opéra Garnier, the centerpiece of the Second Empire.

One of those who happened across the old *pâtisserie* was a chef named François Duthu. "It was rather spooky," he remembers. "It didn't make you want to come inside at all. The saleswomen were dressed in black. It was very sad." Trade had dwindled to the point where there were just a few employees. The oven was still fired by coal, which meant the apprentice had to get up long before dawn to light it so that there would be, as there had been for two and a half centuries, babas.

The cake that made Stohrer rich is a small, plump cake that luxuriates in a sticky bath, decorated with a sprig of angelica. At his court in Lunéville, east of Paris, the exiled King Stanislas I of Poland, who had ruled for just three years, comforted himself for the ensuing thirty years with a raisin brioche soaked in strong liqueur and flambéed, like a plum pudding. Some say he brought a cake with him from Poland, and it had gone hard after the journey. He asked his baker, Stohrer, if he could do anything with it. Stohrer searched for inspiration and soaked the cake in a liqueur. Others claim the cake was a *Kugelhopf*, a raisin brioche for which the village of Lemberg, near Lunéville in the foothills of the Vosges, was renowned. However, Alexandre Dumas insists he learned from the Countess Risleff, a descendant of the king, that the real Polish baba was made with rye flour and soaked in Hungarian Tokay wine. At any rate, in 1725, the king's daughter married Louis XV, and she brought with her to Versailles her father's baker, Stohrer.

Noticing the appetite of Parisians for pastries, Stohrer soon set himself up selling babas. They were kept wrapped in linen and dunked in a punch made with Malaga or Madeira wine as they were sold, an amusing, esoteric ritual. Liqueurs had a medicinal reputation and there was, as well as royal fame, mystery in Stohrer's syrup. At some point, sugarcane alcohol supplanted fortified wines, and the baba became the rum baba.

Writing in his *Dictionary of Cuisine* 150 years later, Dumas disdained "the little babas that one sees in Paris that dry too easily for approval." A real baba, according to Dumas, should be big enough to be a centerpiece and last several days. It should be made with flaked almonds and raisins (not just any raisins, but *muscat de Malaga*). He agreed with Carême's recommendation that it should be served with a *saucière* full of sweetened Malaga wine.

Dumas was a friend of the *frères* Julien, darlings of Parisian society, whose savarin was a version of the baba soaked in their house liqueur. Dumas dubbed the three burly and bearded brothers the giants of *pâtisserie*. They were jolly and contented cake makers who cultivated a commercial profile. In the Théâtre du Vaudeville near their *maison,* the brothers were the subject of numerous farces. Arthur, Auguste, and Narcisse were caricatured as three large lobsters under a single toque. Good nineteenth-century paternalists, they preached economy and hygiene and helped their employees to start up in business. It's interesting to note that as *pâtissiers* they achieved wealth, fame, and respect. They became the patrons of orphanages and board members of friendly societies. And they owed it all to the savarin. Auguste Julien had worked in the *maison* of Stohrer and knew there was a fortune in the flavor that came from moistening a cake with a rich, alcoholic syrup. When they opened their own *maison* in 1843, on a corner of the Place de la Bourse, they offered to the public the savarin in its unique syrup, followed by such famous *gâteaux* as the *pensée,* the *richelieu,* and the *trois-frères.*

Such was the reputation of the savarin *de la Bourse* that some *pâtissiers* sent their sons to work *chez* Julien to steal the secret of their syrup. Others came up with their own variations. The syrup for the *gorenflot,* the speciality of the *maison* of Bourbonneux, was a heady blend of anise and absinthe. It was used to annoint a cake christened after the famous monk who sold cakes in the courtyard of the Louvre when he wasn't confessing the young courtiers of Henry III.

But there was only one savarin. The liqueurs used were mixed in the presence of one of the three brothers by a distiller friend, after which the barrels were brought to Paris. They contained kirsch, anisette, *eau de noyau,* curaçao, and vanilla essence. By the time the last of the brothers, Narcisse, had died in 1890, said Pierre Lacam, "There wasn't a *soirée* at which one didn't serve a savarin, either hot or iced." Of the *maison* of Julien, which moved to Rue du Pont Louis-Philippe, only the decor remains, preserved in what is now a restaurant.

François Duthu was a chef at a large Paris hotel when he first came across Stohrer, which had somehow survived the changing fashions of the nineteenth century and was still selling its little rum babas. He was determined to rescue the venerable *pâtisserie:* "It was interesting to take over somewhere like this. There aren't many places like it in Paris." With a management partner, he bought the premises. They refurbished the kitchens but kept the original features of the shop. In the vaulted cellars they found old hand-hammered iron molds. No one knew what cakes they were for. "They were molds used by *oublayeurs,"* says François. *Oublies* were wafers cooked between hot irons. "It was like the Middle Ages in here."

François's father was a farmer in the Pyrenees, and the son used to cook at home for the family. "When it was time to decide on a trade, well, I liked to eat, I liked the taste of things. . ." At the age of thirteen he was sent to the École Hotelier at Lourdes, for three years. He cooked in a local restaurant for a year before coming to Paris, where he worked his way up the ranks in the kitchens of a large hotel before changing uniforms to become a head waiter. "It's very difficult for a chef to go into business straightaway, if he hasn't been outside of the kitchen," he says. "Here I'm more often in the *boutique* than in the kitchen, taking orders and so on. When the products leave, you have to see them, see that a cake isn't damaged when you put it in the box, that it's perfect, finished. I like that. You can explain how the cake is made. Customers always like to know."

A pastry chef is a person of particular skills. As a chef, François was confident that he could supervise the preparation of the savories—*pâtés en croute, friands,* and so on—that comprise half of their business. For the *pâtisserie* he wanted someone devoted to the art. The master *pâtissier* at Stohrer who is also a *chocolatier* and *glacier,* adept in the making of sweets and ice creams—is forty-six-year-old Claude Moreau. He comes from a family of masons in Normandy, and joined Stohrer after seven years at the estimable *maison* of Peltier, whose cakes have an impeccable perfection of presentation. Peltier established a branch in Tokyo, and Claude worked there adapting recipes to Japanese tastes and local ingredients. He is a soft-spoken, meticulous man, and confesses his favorite culinary activity is the preparation of simple croissants.

"I'm a gourmand!" Claude jokes, meaning that he loves all food, not just the exquisite foods that appeal to gourmets. He likes to make croissants because "it's a nice material, flaky pastry, pleasant to work with. And you know what you're going to get; it's the result of a process."

In the kitchens of Stohrer, he is preparing a batch of babas. He explains that the dough is like that for a brioche but less rich: "Not too much butter or too many eggs, or it will be crumbly and break up when it's soaked." He begins by mixing together the flour, water, and eggs. "The pastry must be elastic; you need a flour with a high gluten content." He mixes the salt and sugar together with a little water and adds that. "The sequence is important. Otherwise you kill the elements." He then adds the yeast dissolved in some warm water.

Claude Moreau, master *pâtissier* at Stohrer, removing babas baked to perfection.

He kneads the pastry by lifting and folding it over. "You must make the pastry strong, rolling it over and not breaking it." When the pastry begins to "slap" on the counter, he adds the melted butter. "But wait for the butter to be completely cold before adding it." With his fingers drawn together, Claude takes a dollop of the sticky pastry and lets it fall slowly into the mold. Patience is vital. "Until you get used to it," he admits, "it goes everywhere."

The pastry should be left to rise for twenty minutes, until it triples in volume. Then it should go straight into the oven for forty minutes. It will have a dry aspect when it comes out. The next day, it can be dunked. "It has to *drink* the rum, head first!" says Claude.

Down in the cellars of Stohrer there was also a pile of molds for another house speciality. These black iron squares are now in use making *puits d'amour,* a pastry reputedly devised by Stohrer. The name alone, which means "well of love," is delectable enough. It's a kind of *vol-au-vent* that used to be filled with red currant jelly—until the 1920s, when *crème pâtissière* came to be used instead—and caramelized on top. Around the same time, the former owner of Stohrer had the square molds specially made in various sizes so as to standardize the quantity of custard. Some *pâtissiers* sell *puits d'amour* made with a base of flaky pastry and a ring of choux. It takes less trouble, but it's not an authentic *puit d'amour.*

"You need a special mold to make it," says François Duthu, "because it's made upside down. Then you need *crème pâtissière,* which has to be cooked exactly right. And the caramel has to be burnt with an iron that's very hot, red hot. It's hard to manage at home." He apologizes for this. "You have to go to a *pâtissier!"*

For a *puit d'amour,* there are customers who come to Stohrer from as far away as Switzerland. But as well as millionaires, there are tramps from the neighborhood who come to buy something everyday. "Perhaps not cakes, but a sandwich," says François Duthu, who is proud to have saved part of the French culinary patrimony. There are thirty staff working behind the little shopfront, and the *maison* is thriving. But he is anxious about the future:

"There aren't many *pâtissiers* left. The profession hasn't grown at all because people buy more and more frozen products. Slowly, they will lose the taste. But the real problem is that it's harder and harder to find qualified people." He is not optimistic about the future. "In a few decades it'll be impossible. It'll be a real luxury to be able to afford a good *gâteau*, handmade by a *pâtissier*. There will always be a demand—anyone who's used to something good will travel a long way to find it again—but there has to be someone there to make it. You can't make it with a machine; it's not possible."

The profession is threatened, François thinks, because it's one that demands devotion. "It's considered inferior to enter a trade, a manual trade, via an apprenticeship. It's not valued, though it's well paid. Once it becomes hard to find people, you have to pay them well. Our people are better paid than those who do eight hours in an office but the eight hours here might be in the evening or on weekends. And especially during holidays. We work while others play and because we're a society of leisure now, people don't want to work on Saturdays and Sundays and holidays. These are our best days. Christmas is the time we're busiest.

"Fifteen years ago it wasn't like that. When I was young and it was time to decide on a trade, becoming a chef was something honorable. Many of our apprentices come from the provinces, like me. But in a few years there won't be many traditional *pâtissiers* like us left. As for us, we'll continue because of the name. Stohrer has to survive. I'll fight for that."

*P*âtissiers are artists of the ephemeral, and their great *maisons*—edifices built of flour, cream, and sugar—usually don't survive. There is a personal character to *pâtisserie* that seemingly can't be passed from master to apprentice. For this reason, *pâtisserie* is always being reinvented. Only in recent decades have industrial processes been available to *pâtissiers* like Gaston Lenôtre, assuring them deep-frozen immortality.

If frozen *gâteaux,* even from Lenôtre, draw mixed reviews (they'll never be as good as fresh, handmade ones but they *are* convenient), they aren't really a threat to the continuity of French cake and pastry making. François Duthu has voiced the greater worry of *pâtissiers* and *boulangers* alike, who wonder how their professions will evolve as apprentices become increasingly difficult to find.

France still has more bakers per capita than any other country. And the French eat more bread than any other nation (though not enough for the union of *boulangers,* who complain that their compatriots eat less than before). There are *boulangeries* everywhere, on every corner: old ones with paint peeling from the window frames and cracked panes of frosted glass separating the *fournil* from the *boutique;* and new ones refurbished in glitter-flecked vinyl with piped lighting that usually sell pastries and sandwiches (the source of funds for their facelifts), as well as a wide variety of breads. France is an outdoor museum of *boulangeries.* Old or new, they seem to have been there forever, so much are they a part of the life of the neighborhood.

For every exclusive *pâtisserie* like Stohrer, there are a dozen *boulangeries.* Bakers are less important than are their *boulangeries,* which might change ownership but really belong to their customers. The only traces of the bakers might be the signatures they leave by the doors of the ovens. During the Second Empire, there were just nine hundred *boulangeries* in Paris. When the First World War ended, there were 2,800, a bakery for every 1,300 people. These modest *affaires* had painted glass panels depicting wispy *semeuses* and rosy maidens busy at the harvest. Beautifully etched golden wheat sheaves and ears of barleycorn served as motifs for price lists. The hours at which *viennoiserie* and croissants came hot from the oven were drawn to the attention of customers. Bread emerged crackling from the ovens without cease. And there was always a *boulangerie* open, for finding one closed would stir deep anxieties. Indeed, there is an agreement between neighboring *boulangeries* that they will not all shut at the same time. They stagger closing days and holidays, notifying the town hall and posting their schedules on official bulletin boards so that no one will be without their daily bread.

The painted panels and engraved windows that decorate *boulangeries* often carry a signature, though they weren't the work of individuals. The names in script are those of the *atelier,* or studio. The most common is Benoist et Fils, a company that decorated at least 180 *boulangeries* in the Paris region, as well as 40 *charcuteries* and 30 *crémeries.* The family company was active for three generations, between 1885 and 1936, decades of increasing prosperity for *boulangers,* who could afford to renovate in high style.

The firm was founded by Maximilien-Louis Benoist, born in Brussels in 1830. It's not known if he studied art, but he evidently had a good command of the salon style and a great finesse in execution. Of all the family he was perhaps the most gifted artist, and eventually retired to paint landscapes at their summer house in Brittany. He started by making sun blinds for shops that were decorated with "attributes, landscapes, figures, flowers, etc." His first clients were *charcuteries,* but by the time his son Théophile took over in 1900, Benoist et Fils was specializing in the decoration of *boulangeries.* Théophile reputedly attended

A cornucopia of loaves on a glass panel by Benoist *père*.
The decorative work of this family firm on hundreds
of *boulangeries* in Paris and the provinces has fallen into ruin.

the École des Beaux Arts, though his name doesn't figure on the rolls of pupils. Like his father, he painted landscapes for pleasure. He was known in the studio—where a telephone was installed but not electricity as he didn't like artificial light—for his painstaking depictions of water mills.

Scenes of labor in the fields and bucolic bounty characterized the panels and ceilings of shops fitted by Benoist et Fils. Wheat sheaves were a common motif; maidens scattering grain and old men reaping the harvest were usual. The pictures were painted on the back of glass, which reflected light and facilitated cleaning. The panes were then set in wooden frames on walls or fixed to iron grids on ceilings so that they could be mounted and taken down. The ceilings were versions of baroque skies, with clouds and cherubs against a deep blue preferred by Louis Benoist. Since they were less prone to damage, many have survived.

The longest-standing employee of the Benoist family was the "installer," known as Jean-Jean, who was with them until 1930. In a photo from 1910, the personnel of the studio can be seen, wearing white smocks and string-ties: the letterer; the *fleuriste,* who painted only flowers; the *maroufleur,* nicknamed Soleil (who was a deaf-mute, and worked for many years for the family stretching and gluing the canvases to glass); the *doreuse* (women usually did the fine gold-leaf work); and the decorator, who painted the frames and walls once the panels were in place.

Theophile's son George-Louis did attend art school, but only twice a week. Like his father, he was good at fine, detailed work, especially with gold leaf. After the First World War, fashions changed. The style established by his grandfather during the Belle Époque was no longer popular. George-Louis finally sold the *atelier* in 1945 and became a scene painter for television. Many of the panels and ceilings of Benoist have been preserved by the Museum of Arts and Traditions. And many more can still be seen while buying a loaf of bread.

The French are regaled by the efforts of their *boulangers,* whom they regard in return with a wariness rooted in age-old mistrust. So-and-so's bread is not as good as another's, or not as good as it used to be. As customers they are fierce, knowledgeable critics, and great connoisseurs: Tell them you're writing a book about bread, and they will tell you with proprietorial satisfaction of an excellent *boulanger* right around the corner from where they live.

A delicate balance of forces preserves these independent bakers. Elsewhere in northern Europe and in the United States, the balance long ago tilted in favor of bakery chains and supermarkets that sell a standardized product. Their customers have forgotten what handmade, idiosyncratic bread tastes like and, out of boredom, eat less of the mediocre bread that is widely available.

Why is French bread so good? One reason is that the price of a basic loaf has been controlled one way or another from the days of King Dagobert, ruler of the Francs in the seventh century. Charlemagne saw to it that the number of bakers in a town was maintained by the hiring of apprentices. The point of a thousand years of royal decrees, and two hundred years of republican ones, was to ensure the availability of an affordable loaf of bread. Since a loaf of the same weight and price, baked from much the same flour, could be bought anywhere, the only way a *boulanger* could increase his takings was by baking a better-tasting loaf. In this way, a precious expertise was gained in France.

The price of a basic loaf was finally deregulated in the 1980s under President Mitterrand. The price of a baguette rose by a few centimes, and a slight grumbling was heard among the populace, giving the Jacobin government some moments of historical unease. But the murmurs subsided and nothing seemed to change.

In the shopping malls and supermarkets, however, a new kind of *boulangerie* opened, known in the profession as a *point de cuisson,* a cooking terminal. Dough is delivered already risen and machines load it into automated ovens. Baguettes are sold cheaply, at or below cost price, as a convenience to attract shoppers. The same equipment can be installed in a *boulangerie,* reducing costs. Although baking is still done on the premises, it's no longer really a bakery but an outlet.

Deregulation permitted price cutting, although as yet there have been no price wars. A tacit consensus—perhaps the result of ancestral memories of famine and turmoil—has kept prices roughly in line, rising by the same amount everywhere. Independent bakers haven't been squeezed out but, finding no artisan to take over when they retire, sell their bakeries to food technicians associated with marketing strategists. The old *boulangerie* is redecorated and opens again as a smart new outlet for bread that is baked in a factory elsewhere, part of a chain with a name that smacks of medieval authenticity, such as The Stone Oven.

Why is French bread so good? Another reason is that it's always fresh. Preservatives are banned. If you see a loaf in a plastic bag, it's being sold cheap for toasting because it's a day or so old. In medieval times, bakers from surrounding villages who brought bread to the markets of Paris had to sell it all the same morning. They weren't allowed to return with any loaves to sell again at the next market. Fresh bread has a short shelf life, and regular demand and labor is required to produce it.

Demand is not a problem. The appetite of the French for their daily bread, even if it has declined, is insatiable. Factory-made bread has come late to France. Although it's supplanting the products of the average baker and replacing them with an average product, good bakers still thrive. Everyone knows of a good baker, not too far away. These are easy enough to identify without even asking. It's outside the *bon boulanger* that the lines form every day.

But the good baker complains that he can't find suitable apprentices: youngsters who are willing to work hard, who have a flair for what is, despite modern methods, the alchemy of baking. The labor needed to make French bread is becoming scarce.

It has been so for a while. In 1973, the sociologist Daniel Bertaux and his wife, Isabelle, conducted interviews with more than a hundred *boulangers*. He found them, first of all, to be suspicious: "I had to be careful what I said. They often thought I was from the government, a kind of tax inspector, and they told their wives to tell me they were out." He was interested in *boulangeries* as an example of social relations that had disappeared in many areas. At the back of his mind was the question, why is French bread so good?

"The taste?" he asks. "The ingredients? No. It's the *boulanger* and the workers who create the taste. They provide the human hands for production. You could do it with industrial methods, but it wouldn't taste the same." In his study, he found that most *boulangers* in Paris come from the provinces. "They come from all the regions of France except Paris. They bring with them expertise in regional types of bread, incidentally, which means you really can find everything in Paris." There is a saying, repeated often enough by *boulangers,* that to be a baker you need to be tough as an ox and just as dumb. "In the old days, sacks of flour weighed two hundred pounds, and the apprentice had to carry them on his back. Before mechanization, strong arms were required to knead the dough with wooden paddles. It was hard, heavy work." Because France was an agricultural nation, there was a steady supply of farm boys who, like the father of Roland Amon, were accustomed to early mornings and the hard work required to achieve the social advancement of becoming a *boulanger.*

Daniel and his wife became aware of the aspirations of *boulangers*. "None of them want their sons to follow them," he says. "They want their sons to become *pâtissiers,* with a successful *maison* in Paris, or to take

It was said you had to be big, strong, and dumb to be a *boulanger:* big to carry
two-hundred-pound sacks of flour, strong to knead the dough, and dumb to work such long hours.
Machines do the kneading now, but it's still said you must have a "feel" for the dough.

up another, easier, more lucrative trade altogether." In the view of *boulangers,* no occupation is more oner-ous than baking bread, which means that *boulangeries* have constantly needed new farm boys to serve as apprentices, and eventually raise the capital to buy out the retiring master baker. This was fine as long as there were farm boys. By the 1970s, though, France was no longer an agricultural nation. Bertaux found that the apprentices he talked to were from the poor, rural regions of southern Europe like Spain and Portu-gal, or from North Africa. "They were immigrants, like the Polish bakers who came here between the wars, prepared to work hard."

Of the provinces, the regions of Brittany and Normandy to the northwest of Paris have been a fertile source of *boulangers.* They are dairy lands producing excellent milk that, mixed with wheat from neighboring Picardy, makes the crepes and galettes for which the region is famous. The best butter in France is an *appellation contrôlée*—a certificate of origin given by the same body that officiates over the names of wines—from the town of Isigny, near Cherbourg in Normandy. If the brioche makes the bakery, it's the butter that makes the brioche. But what makes a baker?

In the gray stone villages of Normandy, tucked away in green valleys, are the *boulangeries* where, like some special harvest, bakers are nurtured. (To a lesser extent, the same is true of villages to the east of Paris, in Alsace, where the chemistry of baking with brewer's yeast first came to France.) As Paris draws suste-nance from the wheat fields that surround it, so it has also drawn the talents of bakers. Bernard Boisguerin, a *boulanger* from the village of Ambonnay in Normandy, confirms the conclusions of Daniel Bertaux, though it seems to him a long time since he left Normandy for Paris. He owns his own *boulangerie* now, and is ceaselessly, methodically rolling out pastry for the weekend's croissants as he talks. He puts the sheets of

Bernard Boisguerin took over this 150-year-old bakery at Choisy-le-Roi,
in the suburbs of Paris. The specialties—*bouchées à la reine,
petit fours,* and croissants—are still available.

pastry through what looks like a wringer, back and forth four times. He cuts, rolls, and sets on trays croissant after croissant, gestures he has been repeating for thirty-five years.

"It's a profession where you mustn't be afraid of work," he says. "And country people aren't afraid of work. What's so special about Normandy that it produces bakers? What happens to the fellow from the Auvergne when he comes to Paris? He goes into the cafés and restaurants. They're people who like their clientele; they're jovial, and their customers like them. The Auvergnat is a *bon-vivant*. He has a natural rapport with the profession. The Breton peasant or the Norman peasant arrives in Paris. . . . They have broad backs. Their shoulders were made for kneading dough."

As if to prove the point, Bernard Boisguerin is himself a large, burly man, with a dense gray moustache under which protrudes a smoldering yellow Gauloise. His mother was a cook in the kitchens of a chateau where his father was the gardener. The family lived in the village. "We didn't have electricity. The first time I saw a car I was twelve years old. We didn't have TV. We used to sit next to the wireless and look at it while we listened! We thought it was sensational."

Bernard used to enjoy helping his mother prepare the cakes, and so at age fourteen he became an apprentice *pâtissier* in a bakery in the nearby town of Evreux. The apprenticeship was found through the local newspaper. To this day, he finds his apprentices by placing an advertisement saying *"Cherche apprenti pâtissier,"* exactly like the one his parents answered in the same newspaper.

With five other apprentices he worked twenty hours a day, for six days a week. "And we got kicked in the pants!" It was a typical introduction to the profession. He still recalls the smell of the *plonge,* the sink for washing utensils thick with cream, fat, sugar, and lemons bobbing on top. As a new apprentice, he was made to fish in it if something was needed. He had to deliver the croissants to cafés in the morning, tormented by the warm, buttery smell. He would gather crumbs to eat from the bottom of the basket, nearly fainting from lack of sleep.

"The boss was a real *salaud!* He made us work like slaves," Bernard adds. "I started at 3:00 A.M. and finished at 10:00 P.M. And what's more, he used to tell me off! He complained that I wasn't working hard enough! It was exploitation, pure and simple, like working in a mine or up a chimney. And that was thirty years ago. I used to make my apprentices work twelve or fourteen hours a day, not eighteen. I thought it was normal because that's what they did to me. Now it's eight hours. That's the limit."

He was happy, however, because he liked baking. "It's like a pretty girl. You know if it will happen or not. After fifteen days, I knew. I succeeded in making things. Half of the apprentice *pâtissiers* give up because they're incapable of doing the job. You must have the touch, the gift for decoration and presentation, for getting the recipes right, everything. A *boulanger*. . . . Hah! Look at him. . . ." He nods at an apprentice, a thickset, cheerful young man whom he found through the Normandy newspaper. "He'll always be able to do it. There's water, salt, yeast. Okay? They used to say to be a *boulanger* you must be big, strong, and dumb, because if you were smart you wouldn't do that job! It was very hard; you had to knead with your arms. In the old days there'd be four of them around the kneading tub, big as rugby players. I've heard it said since I was a kid, 'If you want to be a *boulanger,* you'll have to be big, strong, and dumb.'"

That wasn't the only piece of folk wisdom about bakers and bread to come from the northern regions of France. The delicate operation of baking, with its many variables, some evident and others unseen, needed explanation. The transformation of wheat into bread gave rise to many superstitions:

In Brittany, the farmer's wife had to start kneading the dough with her left hand, making the sign of the cross with her right. Once finished, she had to cover the dough and take care to close the door to the room

A bakery in the village of Avenay in the Champagne region. A church and a *boulangerie* together make a French village. Nowadays the *curé* has often departed, but the *boulanger* is still there.

behind her. If a cat entered, the dough wouldn't rise. A spell cast on a baker, for whatever reason, would have the same effect.

If the baker kneaded his dough without sweating, his loaves would rise by half again in cooking and no one who ate them would have to exert themselves. If sweat fell from his brow into the dough, it wouldn't rise. If he whistled as he worked, anyone who ate his bread would fart.

It was also believed in Brittany that a woman should on no account aid in the construction of an oven, or it wouldn't work. Once an oven was built, care was taken not to spill onto the stones any of the cider drunk in celebration, otherwise the first batch of loaves would be flat, or the stones might crack. The wood to cook the first batch of bread was sprinkled with holy water to ward off evil spirits and bring prosperity. Once the oven was good and hot (determined when all the water in a bottle placed at the mouth had evaporated), an egg was broken at the entrance of the oven to ensure plenty of customers.

In Saint Malo, on the northern coast, it was believed that if the oven collapsed during cooking, a member of the baker's family would perish within the year. If tiles fell off the roof of the oven, the baker or someone close to him would catch pneumonia.

To the ancient rites of baking, Christian injunctions were added. If the baker cursed the *curé* while he was baking, his bread wouldn't rise. If he was in a bad temper and angry at someone, his bread had to be eaten at once because it would quickly go stale. Bread cooked at Easter or Christmas gave the power of speech to animals who ate it, and this was clearly something to be avoided.

It was expressly forbidden to bake on Good Friday. The bread would be black from smoke and ashes. In Gascony, it would make blood appear in the oven and the crumb would turn red. In the Ardennes, bread baked on Good Friday would last for eternity. In Brittany, as well as in western France, in Charente and the

Ardennes, some bread was left in the oven on the night of All Saints, to nourish the dead who returned temporarily.

In Lower Brittany, women said a prayer while they kneaded the dough, beseeching saints Alor and Rioval to double it for the next day. On the Channel coast, they implored the dough to rise by saying:

>The leaven in you has risen,
>Now you do the same.
>The wheat from which you came has risen,
>And to harvest it
>Many people have risen,
>The baker, to make you, has risen,
>Now you do the same.

After three years as an apprentice, Bernard Boisguerin took the exam for his *Certificat d'aptitude professionnel.* He was seventeen years old and ready to embark on his career. There was one hitch, however: "Once the apprenticeship was over, I knew nothing at all. I didn't know how to make a single thing. I saw an ad in the paper: *pâtissier* wanted. I worked for two days. Get out! Another ad, two days. Get out!"

Realizing the shortcomings of his provincial beginnings, he did the only thing possible. He left for Paris. A fellow *pâtissier* dropped him off at a Metro station at six in the morning. Boisguerin had no idea what the Metro was. "In Normandy, I had to walk eight kilometers to go to the cinema. I'd been three times. I was too tired to go when I was an apprentice." On Sunday afternoons, when work was over, he would fall asleep and wouldn't wake up until 3:00 A.M. on Tuesday morning, when it was time to start again.

The Paris he arrived in was the one that had been filmed by Pierre Prevert a few years earlier for a delightful short called *Paris mange son pain*. It shows every possible type of Parisian—children, dogs, birds, tramps—eating their bread in every possible way: chewing it, dunking it, picking at it, and floating chunks of it in bowls of warm milk, the way it used to be eaten for breakfast in the country. "The menu of Paris is a song, and bread is the chorus," narrated Jacques Prevert. The romance of Paris was not lost on Bernard Boisguerin; it was soon after he arrived that he met his wife. But they found life hard there, and left soon after for Nice, on the Riviera. "I went with my new wife, hitchhiking," he said. "The next day I started knocking on doors. Do you need a pastry chef? There I met a grand *pâtissier,* Poussec, who took a liking to me. That's when I began to learn. After three months he took a holiday and left me in charge. We stayed there for a year and a half and then my wife got a job in Paris so we came back."

He worked for different *patrons* for fifteen years, including one who, for two months of the year when a big, roving outdoor fair came to Paris, supplied six thousand baguettes a day for the sandwich stands. "My wife thought I was having fun! I started in the morning at 1:00 A.M. and came home at 6:00 P.M. Now she's in the business, she knows what it's like. At first she didn't believe me!"

His wife laughs at this, and rolls her eyes in weary acceptance.

"They say work doesn't kill you but . . ." He lifts the leg of his houndstooth *laboratoire* pants to show his mottled, dry shins. "Look at that, from the heat of the ovens." It was for protection against this affliction that bakers used to pray to Saint Lazarus. "But I was lucky. I was with good *patrons.* I liked what I was doing. After working for eighteen hours I would go out to the front of the shop and look at my cakes. I felt a love for what I did. I was tired but I was content. I think there aren't many people who know what it's like to be happy like that."

The moment finally came for Bernard to go into business for himself. A friend whom he had known as a fellow journeyman baker came to see him and said he was quitting. He offered to sell him his *maison,* but Bernard had no money. The friend said it didn't matter. He could pay him back bit by bit. Next, they went to see the Grand Moulin de Paris. Uncle Farine (whom we have already met) worked out a deal. "He telephoned the boss of the mill and they advanced me the flour the same afternoon." Right away, the profits began to flow. Soon he found himself with twenty-six employees and two *affaires.* Ten years later, he sold them. "I was fed up. It wasn't the baking; it was the paperwork, all the employees." He decided to buy a farm. "It was my dream as a boy to have a farm with cattle, cows, pigs, chickens, rabbits, everything, horses even. I spent half my savings in one year. I made a bad investment. You should stick with what you know. I've still got the farm, but I sold the animals."

All the while, he has been rolling croissants.

"I missed it. It's true. . . ."

He arranges the last one on a tray, neatly spaced beside the others, and takes it to the refrigerator.

"It's a drug. I admit it. It's well known. *Le virus du métier.* You don't have to look far for the reason."

"You've got chocolate on your moustache," says his wife, removing the dark brown speck with a cloth.

"Fifteen years ago, I made money," he confides, "but now I have to be very careful. One too many employees, and you can sink. And it's hard to get apprentices now. The lack of professional conscience is *flagrant!* Young people don't want to work in bakeries because the hours are too long and the rewards too small."

In his bakery at Choisy-le-Roi on the banks of the Seine, Bernard Boisguerin sells a special loaf that he calls *pain d'autrefois.* It's flat and dark brown, a sourdough loaf that's all crust and almost no crumb.

Bazin on the Rue de Charenton, Paris. This neighborhood *boulangerie* was decorated
more than a century ago with customary scenes of sowing and reaping the harvest.

Boulangers take special pride in crusts. Often, it's the only part of a loaf they will eat themselves, but the reasons have as much to do with commerce as taste. The crust is simply the *boulanger's* best advertisement. The textures of a good crust, with its intricate, warm harvest tones, rich as an autumn landscape, are irresistible. The stiff crust serves to carry other foods to the mouth, and chewing the roasted wheat generates saliva for digestion—part of the genius of the sandwich, if not of bread itself. To bake a loaf that's mostly crust with just the lightest of crumb, full of the irregular, cavernous holes that are the sign of proper rising, is the ambition of all *boulangers*. (Customers reject instinctively any bread that has been loath to swell; it seems unripened and might well be indigestible to the lazy chewers we have all become. A big loaf, even if it's full of air, appears to be better value than a small one.)

The crust of Bernard Boisguerin's *pain d'autrefois,* a name that means old-time bread, is almost black. The crumb is virtually nonexistent, just a series of hollow golden caverns in which you can see the crust from the inside. He began baking it after a rep came by selling the ready-mixed dough for a patented loaf. "It was 80 percent water," he explains. "I tried it myself and bit by bit I got there. The secret is the fermentation. You have to take your time. Too much brewer's yeast eats the sugars in the flour." It is, of course, a country-style loaf, though any remaining peasants would consider themselves cheated by the volume of air and require a loaf weighing five times as much. He bakes 250 of them a week in his suburban bakery for restaurants eager for culinary novelty.

Since the 1970s there has been a change in the French attitude to bread. Almost the morning after they finally became an urban rather than a rural people, the French began to yearn for old-fashioned country tastes. Instead of white bread, they wanted bread that tasted like bread, with a hard crust that had the smell of wood smoke, and a crumb that was brown and sour, without being acid. Lionel Poilâne became the most famous baker in France by creating such a loaf, which he patented and sells from his bakery and through subsidiaries as *pain poilâne*. Because it lasts for three weeks rather than three hours, it has the very urban virtue of good shelf life. The highest accolade awarded to *pain poilâne* came after the restaurant cars of French trains were shunted onto sidings for the last time. Meals are no longer served on the new high-speed trains, only sandwiches made from *pain poilâne*.

From his position at the summit of the brotherhood of *boulangers,* Lionel Poilâne deplores his fellow bakers. "They are alchemists in reverse," he complains. "They take gold and they turn out rubbish." Despite this harsh judgment, it wasn't long before every *boulanger* was baking his own version of Poilâne's bread and calling it simply a *pain au levain.* But Poilâne has a point. It is rarely as good as his bread. One reason is that few other than Poilâne use the troublesome wood-burning ovens that give a smoky taste to the bread, complementing the bitterness of the leaven.

Ironically, Lionel Poilâne's "country-style" bread became popular in the cities just as it finally disappeared from the countryside. Distanced from their past, people in the cities wanted a product with history. This kind of bread has a culinary, a cultural, and even a biological history in the spores that enter the dough from the air—and from the sweat of the baker's hands as he kneads. *Pain au levain* is bread as it used to be, with irregular holes in the crumb and bits of charred wood from the fire embedded underneath.

The fashion for *pain au levain* and *pain de campagne*—so-called "country bread"—has been part of the search for authenticity and character in a world where tastes have been homogenized. People wondered if something were wrong with *them* when everything began to taste the same. Far from the old village, they couldn't raise the matter with the baker, or even the supermarket manager, and complained to their psychiatrist instead. There is an old French proverb: "Better to run to the baker than the doctor." Bread, after all, used to be life. It wasn't life that had become insipid. The millions of baguettes all tasted the same because the same prerisen refrigerated dough is delivered by tanker trucks to bakers who simply connect a large tube to the same machines that roll out and bake them.

Eventually, the government had to intervene; it gave a legal definition for two new categories of loaf. If the dough is mixed, kneaded, risen, and baked on the premises, the loaf can be called *pain de maison*. If the dough has been prepared off-premises, but has not been deep frozen and contains no additives, it can be labelled *pain de fabrication française*. Once upon a time, French customers would have been able to tell the difference.

Country-style loaves are thought to be more wholesome because they're made with rough-milled whole-grain flour. Yet their fabrication is just as streamlined as that of any other loaf. They still contain some fiber, which is good for digestion, but the germ oil, which contains most of the nutritives, is usually extracted to prevent the flour from going rancid too easily. In 1969, the Grand Moulin de Paris started selling what they termed a "mix." These combine different cereals, or cereals milled to different grades, ready for baking into whole wheat loaves, bran loaves, and the like. In the 1970s, German mills became the specialists at these combinations, supplying many French *boulangeries* with mixes for the rustic types of bread traditional to Germany. From a few individual bakers the fashion has spread. As the independent artisans retire, bakery chains are springing up—but they are chains of gourmet bakers *à la française* that sell "country-style" loaves made from industrial mixes. A chain called the Fournil de Pierre—The Stone Oven—is a notable example. The decor is quasi-medieval: wooden beams and iron grilles. The pale, earthy tones of the bare brick walls suggest the naturalness of the product. And the oven is framed by a stone arch, though it's fired by gas and lined with bricks, like any other modern oven.

One entrepreneur who confesses he was bitten by bread has tried to preserve old *boulangeries,* creating a chain by changing only their names and the kinds of loaves they sell. "Bread is not just a business," bemoans Basil Kamir, "It's an obsession!" The bread available in the three Paris branches of his Moulin de la Vierge is made with flour from the Decollogne-Lecocq mill in the Marne valley, organically grown and ground by local burr stones. Jean-Luc Poujauran uses the same flour in his bakery, and the range of bread in the Moulin de la Vierge is similar. Twenty years ago, such loaves would have been found only on a hippie commune, baked by amateurs obsessed with the purity of the ingredients, and eaten with honey and fresh goat's cheese. Now they're baked by the best *boulangers,* who have an epicurean rather than political obsession with their ingredients.

oulangers bemoan standardization and decry the demise of the artisan. But what they would really **B**like to do is patent a loaf.

Like Lionel Poilâne, Jean-Luc Poujauran has patented a loaf. It's a called a Painwich, a loaf of bread shaped like a chef's toque that has been hollowed out and baked using special molds he designed himself. It can be filled with food and the top replaced. He has licensed it to the *Train Bleu,* the famous restaurant in the Gare de Lyon, which serves a *coq-au-vin* in a Painwich for people who are in a hurry to catch departing high-speed trains and for those who are bored with Poilâne's sandwiches.

It was inevitable that, sooner or later, such ingenuity would get around to the baguette, which after all is a descendent of *pain mollet,* named for a *boulanger* who lived six hundred years ago on the Rue des Arcis, and who was reputed to have baked the whitest loaf in Paris.

The *boulanger* who set out to bake a better baguette was *maître* Ganachaud. Bernard Boisguerin worked for him, and considers him to be one of the *boulangers* who popularized "country-style" bread in France. He retired a few years ago, but his legacy is the *flûte Gana,* a baguette of incomparable lightness, with a golden, fulsome crust, whose methods of fabrication he has patented. It's a baguette with something of the sour taste and the shelf life of a *pain de campagne,* though the crumb is smooth and creamy white. It has one other virtue for the twenty or so bakers who sell it: It is almost twice the price of a baguette. The dough is raised using a technique known as *sur poulish,* which is also reputed to produce the best *viennoiserie.* It's an old Polish method of raising dough slowly, by starting with a small amount of brewer's yeast and using a lot of water. The resulting leaven has the consistency of a pancake mix. (This is but one example of the considerable ingenuity that Polish immigrants have brought to French baking. Indeed, the father of Lionel Poilâne was a baker who emigrated from Poland.)

Ganachaud's bakery is still thriving, located in a crowded district of old Paris not far from Edith Piaf's birthplace. Every evening as people return from work, long lines form outside the bakery, one of the busiest in Paris. Ganachaud had it rebuilt in the early 1970s in a mock medieval style, with bare brick and heavy timber and iron railings that bow out into the street. Behind the bowed grilles, fresh-baked loaves are set out. On one wall is an illuminated reproduction of a famous illustration of a medieval *boulangerie,* colored to resemble stained glass. In the kitchens downstairs, there are the usual tall refrigerators for raising dough and four specially built large ovens. These are circular, with floors that rotate slowly to allow continuous loading and unloading. Everywhere are folds of jute, known as *couches,* for the loaves. It's on these cloths that the dough is left to rise and the loaves to cool after baking.

The bakery has been bought by Jean Jeudon, a master *boulanger* who was a friend of Ganachaud and wanted to perpetuate the traditions of his unique bakery. He is proud of the fact that regular *enfournement* in the rotating ovens means that fresh bread is available, hot, for the two thousand customers who come every day, and he winces at the mention of microwave ovens that are used elsewhere. Ganachaud sells thirty kinds of loaves made by eight different methods of raising. Among them are the *tordu,* a twisted loaf from Gers, and *tougnole* from the Pyrenees, a loaf enriched with wheat germ, as well as loaves made with rye flour and raisins, loaves with walnuts, and others with flour classed as *biologique*. This is the French term for organic produce, grown without nitrates, sulfites, or artificial fertilizers. "The hardest thing," says *maître* Jeudon, "is to find a good wheat, because the high-yield wheat that's commonly grown is not the best wheat." After that, it depends on the baker, in his view. "Some mix flour the way you mix plaster. It's never the same. From the inert, we create something living."

Jean Jeudon is a bread purist. He eats a whole baguette himself with every meal. "And sometimes I snack on one during the day, too," he adds. He was born in the valley of the Sarthe, in western Brittany. One of his father's cousins was a *boulanger,* and he was sent to stay with him as a boy. "I remember those days better than anything in my childhood. He had a wood-fired oven and a mechanical *pétrin."* In the same village now there is no longer a *boulanger,* just a *dépôt de pain* selling bread baked in a factory. Although the population is still about a thousand—enough to support a *boulanger*—no one will do the job. "You can't find people to work six days and nights a week. You have to have a passion for it. It's not an ordinary profession."

It's a source of satisfaction to *maître* Jeudon that two-thirds of the turnover in his bakery comes from speciality breads: bran, whole-wheat, rye, and "country-style" loaves, as well as the *flûte Gana.* Just around the corner, Ganachaud's heirs, his two daughters, have opened their own *boulangerie* and named it La Flûte Gana. When Ganachaud retired from the bakery that bears his name, he went to Tokyo for a while to oversee production of his baguette, the perfection of perfection. The Japanese, who appreciate the skilled manipulation of nature towards an ideal, are great admirers of the zen of French baking.

A bakery in the village of Cumières in the Champagne region. The new owners,
Monsieur Roussel and his wife, intend to repaint it exactly as it was last painted thirty years ago.

The old *boulangerie* had become a *dépôt de pain,* like the one in the village where *maître* Jeudon served his apprenticeship. The sight is typical of the quiet villages of the Berry, though it's not a very wealthy region and, therefore, one of the least altered. It's a flat, marshy landscape, located south of the Loire valley. In the window of the old *boulangerie* are glass jars full of purple marshmallows, canned vegetables, pots of yogurt, and biscuits in tins. An old couple sits in the living room, connected by a door to the *boutique.* The door is open and, in the living room, a TV is on. A few loaves stand on a wrought-iron rack, but these were baked elsewhere, across the fields in the nearby town.

For nearly an hour, church bells have been pealing maniacally. When asked why, the old baker laughs. "It's the *curé.* He's crazy. He rings the bells like that every year. There's hardly anyone left in the village to hear them."

The tolling bells signify the annual festival of Joan of Arc, the teenage martyr dear to the people of Orléans, which is the nearest city. Saint Joan liked to dip her bread in wine, but not out of religious fervor. It was an old peasant fortification for a cold morning in the fields. There is a drab silence over the grasslands and no farm laborer in sight. Cocks crow somewhere in reply to the church bells, muffled by a low-pressure belt. Purple flowers damp with dew sprout from the hedges along a lane that leads from the village. There, just outside the village, a communal oven was once located, built of stone, with a tiled roof. The *fournil* was in the open air, located away from any dwellings as a precaution against fire. Twice a week, smoke from the wood fire would pour from the chimney as bread was being baked. But it has now become part of someone's weekend home. The owners bring their bread with them, purchasing it from a market on the outskirts of Orléans.

It's the same in the next village, and the next. In the empty main squares, the *boulangeries* have closed. To buy their daily bread, people travel to the towns. No more baking is done in the *boulangeries,* though many of them are still *boulangeries* and seem as though they are closed for a vacation from which everyone has forgotten to return. The shutters have been bolted or the blinds lowered in the windows and the paintwork is cracked and going slowly gray.

In the mall along the main road from Orléans, however, the *boulangerie* is thriving. Nothing has really changed. The bread is whiter, and blander, but the supply is more reliable and far less effort is involved in procuring it. The decor is even in the popular wood-and-brick mock-medieval style. The old market square has simply been transferred to an enclosed food court. People still encounter their neighbors in the line. They buy a supply for the next few days with habitual concentration, but instead of carrying wicker baskets, they push shopping carts, or carry their baguettes in long paper sacks with a brand-name printed on them.

It's a fact of modern French retail design that if the *boulanger* is good, the mall will thrive. In the new malls of the satellite suburbs, a *boulanger,* usually part of a chain, is considered an anchor tenant. The *boulangeries* are deliberately sited near entrances to let the enticing odors of roasting wheat and caramelizing sugar create an instant mood of warmth and well-being, with ancient connotations of safety and plenty. The baking is done on the premises—it couldn't be otherwise—but the preparation of the dough is done elsewhere, by means of industrial methods.

These methods are not as reckless as they once might have been. At the École de Boulangerie de Paris, run by one of the big milling companies, the instructors take pains to reintegrate "personality" into the baker's product. "It used to take six hours to make bread; now it takes three," explains Jacques Harvard, the agricultural engineer responsible for the course, which trains eighty bakers a year. "But that's been to the detriment of the taste. Like cheese, if it's made in too antiseptic and too hurried a way, it loses the richness of taste. It's a perfect loaf but there's something missing. We try to put a natural touch back into what has unavoidably become an industrial product."

It was in 1969, probably the same year the village baker began thinking about retirement, that, as Jacques Harvard says, "a return to tradition began." Thus, in the *boulangerie* in the mall outside Orléans, a regional speciality is offered, a link with the past, and with nature. It's a *pain aux trois céréales,* made from a mix of wheat, oat, and rye flours; but there is nothing local about it. The mix has come from a mill far away. And nature has been greatly assisted in her efforts—the cereals are grown with the aid of nitrates and milled by metal rollers, cracking the grain and destroying the fiber. Afterward, some lightly milled grains are added to give the impression that the flour has been stone-milled.

The "country" in *pain de campagne* is not specified. It's a country that has become generalized with the loss of its true location. Very little in a *boulangerie* nowadays has a genuine taste of the *terroir*. This word, meaning agricultural region and the concept of being able to taste the soil of origin in a food, is very fashionable now with people nostalgic for their vanished rural past. The brioche once depended for its flavor, and its reputation, on butter from the farms of Normandy or Brie. Now the brioche is everywhere, and few people can tell the difference between butter from Normandy and butter from Charente.

The importance of wheat in France has meant that there is little difference between bread from the different regions. What were once local specialities, like brioches or crepes, have either become popular everywhere or been forgotten. In the Catholic city of Rheims, the capital of the Champagne region, for example, excellent *pain d'épice,* made with honey and spices, is still to be found. It used to be baked exclusively by monks, until any baker could purloin the once-rare spices.

In the rain-washed, gray stone towns of Brittany, milky rich crepes and galettes offer some brightness. Wheat and bread have always been associated with the sun, which ripens the wheat to produce a golden bounty. In early Christian times, a token of this goodness was offered in thanks for the harvest. The old beliefs have persisted in the northwest of France: A piece of galette—unleavened, griddle-cooked bread—is placed on the waters of a brook bearing a candle. If the galette sinks, it is a bad omen.

The smooth, dense *pain brié* of Normandy used to be made with dough thickened like butter with a wooden paddle. A bread with the same name—though relatively light, as it's kneaded with mechanical mixers—can still be found in some towns. *Boulangers* won't risk upsetting the delicate stomachs of their customers, who don't have the patience to chew a bread as dense as *pain brié.*

In the Rhône valley in the southern city of Lyons, *boulangers* baked a "poor man's brioche," *pain de courge,* so-called because the yellow color came not from butter but from the addition of squash. It was popular with the poor mill workers of the old French silk-weaving capital. Lyonnais *boulangers* baked them to give away to hungry urchins who came begging at the end of each day.

In the south of France, bread has a different, Mediterranean character. Far from the plains of wheat surrounding Paris, bread was less ample. Rather than being long, full, and light, loaves typical of the Mediterranean coast of France are round and flat. The olive gives them substance: either whole olives added to the dough for flavor, or olive oil mixed into the dough. Most delicious of all is olive oil simply poured onto fresh bread instead of butter. The cultivation of olives around the Mediterranean is as old as the growing of wheat. Round, flat loaves baked in embers between two metal saucers were found in the tombs of the pharaohs. They were smaller than those sold today around the region, but the strain of wheat used to bake them is the same.

Since bread and cakes will become hard if left in the window, *boulangers* prefer to indulge
in eccentric displays, like this one of family photos at Lacaille on the Avenue de Bel-Air, Paris.

The most famous loaf from the south of France is the *fougasse,* made with second-quality, rougher-textured wheat flour, kneaded and folded into a distinctive shape, rather like a baseball glove. The name comes from the Latin *focacia,* meaning "of the home," and these loaves were once simply homemade bread. Everywhere in the south of France, *boulangers* bake *fougasses* nowadays, adding olives and sometimes anchovies to the dough. In Jean Giono's tale of the baker's unfaithful wife mentioned earlier, it was their daily *fougasse* that the villagers missed. Giono described how his hero awoke from his afternoon nap in the Provençal sun to eat *fougasses* made with anchovy, dipped in a sauce of crushed garlic and wild shallots. In the port of Marseilles, where bread-baking methods first arrived from the eastern Mediterranean, *fougasses* are the loaves baked by every *boulanger.* It's possible to purchase a loaf old as antiquity, baked fresh that morning.

In the valley of Beaufortain, high in the Alpine mountains, there is a communal oven still standing in a village, built more than a century ago but long unused.

The flat valley floor is covered in deep snow. The few trails from cross-country skiers are easy to pick out, and just over the high Beaufort range is Courchevel, once the most fashionable, now merely the largest ski resort in the world. In the valley of Beaufortain, however, the landscape is typical of French agricultural decline, but under snow. The alpine chalets are old and ramshackle and their wooden walls have turned gray-black from lack of attention.

It was through these valleys that the Romans came to France, bringing with them Greek bakers famed for the thirty different kinds of loaves they baked. In a nearby valley is the village of Artas, where until a few hundred years ago there remained the ruins of a temple dedicated to *Artos,* which means bread in Greek.

No bread was baked in the stone oven in Beaufort after the Second World War, when it was replaced by a much smaller iron oven. That, too, soon fell into disuse when the *boulanger* in the nearby town acquired a van and began making delivery rounds. Local people moved away, and the village found itself with a population of just forty-five people.

In the communal oven at Beaufort, bread used to be baked for the shepherds who followed their flocks of sheep up the slopes. Grass grows at different altitudes depending on the season, and the animals used to eat their way up the hillsides. The shepherds followed, taking with them bread that was hard and purple, baked to last a month or more. There are still sheep on the farms, and some dairy herds. The village is holding its own, according to Claude, a dairy farmer who came from Normandy to settle there. "The problem is the young people want to leave, and there's no one to carry on. But people are finding ways," he says. He fears the new monoculture of tourism that fills adjoining valleys with weekend traffic jams, not for environmental reasons, but out of a farmer's instinctive pragmatism about anything that depends on the weather. "If the season is bad and there's no snow, it's a disaster."

After fifteen years Claude gave up dairy farming in Normandy, frustrated by production quotas and fed up at the heavy use of fertilizers. "It was becoming too intensive." Some friends had moved to the Alps to take over a sheep farm, and Claude and his wife decided to join them. Like most small French farmers nowadays, they had to look for ways to supplement their farming income. The old stone oven, still intact in the middle of the village, gave Claude and his wife, Danièle, the idea of baking bread.

As a farmer, he had the right to bake and sell a certain quantity of bread, though it impinged on the trade of local *boulangers*. But it was a hard art to master. "At first the bread was burnt, or too tough," he admits. The oven is primitive. To heat it, burning wood must be placed around the insides of the stone walls. The oven must heat evenly, and there is no thermometer to show when the heat has built sufficiently. It took

A communal oven in the alpine village of Beaufortain. The wood-fired, open-air oven had been cold for half a century when Claude and his wife, Danièle, decided to relight it and bake bread again.

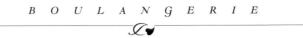

Claude and his wife about two months to get it right, but they were soon selling fifty kilos [about 112 pounds] a week of their *pain au levain*. It has the incomparable taste of a true sourdough bread cooked directly in a wood fire, a taste that only Poilâne has succeeded in reproducing on anything like a large scale. Claude and his wife call the bread they bake and sell to surrounding villages *pain d'antan,* old-style bread. "You have to be careful who you say it to," confides Danièle. "For some it brings bad memories of the war. It's synonymous with the tough, hard bread they ate in those days. But for the young it means organic, whole-grain bread and they like that."

In the twelfth century, the king, later to become the beloved Saint Louis, released *boulangers* in towns from their obligations to feudal lords, and these artisans became part of the new bourgeoisie. Ovens on the outskirts of villages, however, belonged to the *seigneur* on whose land they stood. The locals, having already paid a part of their wheat to the miller, would take their flour to the *boulanger* and in exchange receive bread, minus a part for the baker and another part for the *seigneur*. These ovens were known as *fours banaux,* meaning parish ovens. Although they baked a vital commodity, parish ovens were, until the Revolution, a symbol of dependency. Far from being a quaint rural tradition, parish ovens, like mills, represented the tyrannies of famine and exploitation, as the *seigneur* could demand what he pleased for its use, and the nearest town might be far away.

The oven was usually situated on the edge of the village, or near a river, in case of fire. The one in Beaufort is quite recent, built around 1860, at the center of the clutch of wood-and-stone chalets that comprise the village. It used to be a communal oven, owned by the villagers, so it has a more benign significance than older village ovens, though the type of construction is ancient. It's simply a stone hut with an opening at the back that serves as a chimney and an iron door in front. A cross has been carved into the stones at the lower ledge of the mouth. Baking was a lonely, scary business. Waiting for the dough to rise and stoking the embers alone in the early morning, bakers imagined demons swooping to warm themselves in the flames of the oven. It was customary to throw a bread roll into the fire before baking started. *Voilà pour toi, diable!*

Claude doesn't cross himself before placing his loaves, as was once customary, although, unconscious of any reason other than to let the loaf rise in baking, he makes two slashes on the balls of dough in the sign of a cross. He is intent on not losing the heat from the oven, after having placed burning wood around the inside walls and waited until long orange tongues of flame licked up the stones.

"The oven must be hot," he says, concentrating on placing the loaves so they aren't too close to the flames or to one another.

The locals were bemused at first to see Claude and Danièle rekindling the oven. "When we started, many people smiled," says Danièle. "They were skeptical. But now they like to see the oven alight. It means the village isn't dying."

Not as long it still has its daily bread.

Loaves of *pain de campagne* and a *fougasse* hung by its holes
in the Moulin de la Vierge. Urbanites weary of sophisticated white bread and
yearning for old-fashioned country tastes make a cult of loaves like these.

BREAD

The French don't bake bread at home. (The man who came to service our oven was amazed we would want to use it for that purpose.) With a *boulangerie* on every corner, they don't need to. As a result, an aura of almost masonic mystery surrounds the baking of French bread. The *boulangers* we talked to all said you must acquire a "feel" for dough, that the recipe is only the start. The hardest thing to get right, because it varies with the weather and the quality of the ingredients, is the rising of the dough. Rising takes time and patience—the most expensive things you'll need. Always use unbleached flours, stone-milled if available. There is a difference between French and American flours, but what we've found to be more important is the use of good brewer's yeast. It comes in moist, crumbly gray-brown chunks, and should be kept refrigerated. When exposed to heat, it ferments and quickly goes stale. Not all health stores stock it, as it's used only for baking.

Beginners can take comfort from the fact that French bakers once served eleven-year apprenticeships, but intensive courses at a school run by the Grands Moulins de Paris now turn out qualified *boulangers* in three months. If you have flair, all you perhaps lack is equipment. A domestic oven is not like a professional one with brick walls and steam injectors, though it can be adapted. Let the oven heat at the stated temperature for at least fifteen minutes before baking. Oven thermostats can be unreliable, so use an oven thermometer.

BAGUETTES

Once known as *pain de Paris,* the baguette is the quintessential loaf of French bread, a yard-long stick of sharp crust and cavernous, chewy crumb. The average neighborhood *boulanger* produces up to ten thousand baguettes a week. The flour they use is known as French type 55. American flour has a slightly higher gluten content, and is more finely milled. French flour is unbleached, and by law no preservatives are used in bread baking. Only salt is added to the water, yeast, and flour.

Fermentation creates the flavor; the slower the dough rises, the better the taste. Moisture in the oven allows a final rising of the dough, provoked by the high heat. It also helps form an open-textured crust, with a harvest gold color. The characteristic diagonal slashes across the top of a baguette aren't just decorative; they prevent the loaf from twisting and tearing as carbon dioxide expands violently within as it bakes.

DAY ONE:

1 teaspoon brewer's yeast (available at health food stores)
6 tablespoons lukewarm water
⅔ cup plus 2½ tablespoons unbleached all-purpose flour

DAY TWO:

2 tablespoons brewer's yeast
¼ cup lukewarm water
3¾ cups unbleached all-purpose flour
Scant 2 teaspoons salt
¾ cup plus 1 tablespoon water

Day One: In a medium-size bowl, combine the brewer's yeast and lukewarm water until the yeast is dissolved. Add the flour and stir to combine. Knead to form a dough that's soft to touch but not sticky, about 10 to 15 minutes. Form the dough into a ball and cover with a bowl. This dough constitutes a "starter." Let the starter stand, covered, at room temperature, on the work surface overnight.

Day Two: In a cup combine the brewer's yeast and lukewarm water. In a large bowl, combine the flour and salt with the remaining water. Add the starter from day one and the yeast you have just mixed. Knead until the dough is soft and smooth, and when you poke it with your finger the indentation remains, about 10 minutes. Cover the bowl with a clean kitchen towel and let the dough rise at room temperature until it is 1½ times its original bulk, at least 45 minutes, depending on the temperature in the kitchen.

Place a large heat-proof cup of water on the floor of the oven; then preheat the oven to 500°F (hotter if your oven allows). Flour a baking sheet. Working quickly on a floured work surface, knead the dough again briefly. (Tear off an egg-size piece of dough to use as a starter for the next batch.) Reflour the surface and stretch the dough into a tube about 1 inch thick and as long as your oven will allow. Transfer the loaf to the prepared baking sheet, cover, and let rest in a warm place until slightly risen, about 30 minutes.

With a razor blade, not a knife, make a series of diagonal slashes down the length of the top of the loaf, each about ½ inch deep. Reduce the oven temperature to 450°F and bake for 10 minutes. Reduce the temperature again and bake until the crust is golden brown and the loaf sounds hollow if tapped underneath, about 20 minutes more. Let cool on the baking sheet.

Makes one 2½- to 3-foot-long baguette or two 18-inch-long bâtards.

PAIN AU LEVAIN NATUREL
French-style Sourdough

The description "French-style sourdough" is meant to give an idea of how this bread will taste, since sourdough is uniquely American. The crumb of a *pain au levain* isn't white and even. It ought to be a gray-brown color, with irregular holes and a sour though less acidic taste. The crust should be dark brown with the rich texture of an autumn leaf. Note the use of fermented apple as the yeast, or starter.

1 apple
4¼ cups lukewarm water
1 tablespoon salt
5¾ cups unbleached all-purpose flour
5¼ cups whole wheat flour

Rinse, then press the apple, including the seeds, skin, and core through a blender to extract the juice. Let the apple juice stand in a glass at room temperature until it starts to bubble, about 1 week. (After a day or so, the juice will start to "foam." It will start to bubble about 5 days later.)

Begin to make the bread in the early evening. Pour the lukewarm water into a very large bowl and add the apple juice and salt, stirring to dissolve it. Stir in the flours and work the mixture until a dough forms that doesn't stick to your fingers. Gather the dough into a ball and on a lightly floured surface knead it vigorously for about 5 minutes. Cover the dough with a damp cloth and let it rise at room temperature until it has doubled in bulk, about 3 hours, depending on the temperature of your kitchen.

Punch the dough down, knead it again briefly for about 5 minutes, and cover it with a damp cloth. Let stand at room temperature for about 12 hours, or overnight.

The next morning, punch the dough down, and knead it for about 5 minutes. Divide the dough in half (removing an egg-size piece to use as a starter, instead of fermented apple juice, for the next batch). Shape each half into a round loaf. With a sharp knife cut a cross on the top of each loaf, about ¼ inch deep. Transfer the loaves to a baking sheet and cover them with a cloth. Let stand at room temperature for 2 hours.

Place a large heat-proof cup filled with water on the floor of the oven. Preheat the oven to 500°F (or hotter, if your oven allows). Bake the loaves in the middle of the oven until the crusts are dark brown, or until the loaves sound hollow when tapped on the bottom, about 1 hour.

Turn off the oven and allow the loaves to cool on the baking sheet in the oven with the oven door ajar for 30 minutes.

Makes 2 large loaves, whose flavor will improve the next day.

PAIN DE CAMPAGNE
French Country Bread

The piece of dough you saved for the next day from *Pain au Levain Naturel,* a starter known in France as a *chef* or *mère,* can be used instead of the yeast in this recipe.

3 ½ cups rye flour
3 ½ cups unbleached all-purpose flour
4 cups water
2 teaspoons brewer's yeast (available in health-food stores)
1 tablespoon salt

Begin to make the bread in the early evening. Combine the flours in a medium-size bowl. In a saucepan heat the water until lukewarm. Put the yeast in a large bowl, pour in the lukewarm water, and let stand until foamy. Add the salt and half the combined flours, stir, and cover with a clean cloth. Leave this liquid starter dough in a warm, draft-free place for 24 hours.

The following evening, gradually add the remaining flours and knead the dough in the bowl until it's elastic, about 10 minutes. (When the dough is no longer sticky you have added sufficient flour.) Cover the dough and leave in a warm, draft-free place until it rises to about 1 ½ times original size, about 12 hours.

The next morning, punch down the dough, transfer it to a floured work surface, and divide it in half. Shape round, domed loaves, saving a little dough from each loaf to decorate the top. (Lay two lengths of dough in a cross, for example.) Transfer the loaves to a floured baking sheet and let rise partially, about 3 hours.

Place a large heat-proof cup filled with water on the floor of the oven. Preheat the oven to 500° F (or higher, if your oven allows). Bake the loaves in the lower third of the oven for 10 minutes. Reduce the oven temperature to 425° F and bake until the crust is firm and well colored and the loaves sound hollow when tapped on the bottom, another 50 minutes. Transfer the loaves to wire racks and let them cool completely.

Makes 2 round loaves.

Pain de Son
Whole Wheat Bread with Bran

Once upon a time, *boulangers* in towns had special dispensation to keep pigs to devour the leftover wheat bran. Now bran is prized as roughage, and makes a rich, savory bread.

2 cups lukewarm water
2½ tablespoons brewer's yeast (available in health-food stores)
2 tablespoons firmly packed dark brown sugar
3¾ cups plus 5 tablespoons whole wheat flour
1 cup wheat bran (available in health-food stores)
1 tablespoon olive oil
1 tablespoon salt
2 tablespoons water mixed with pinch of salt
Oat flakes (available in health-food stores)

Pour the lukewarm water into a large bowl. Add the yeast and brown sugar and stir to combine. Let stand until the mixture turns foamy on the surface.

Add the flour and stir it until incorporated. Mix in the bran, olive oil, and salt until thoroughly combined. On a lightly floured surface, knead the dough until it is no longer sticky to the touch, about 15 minutes. Cover with a cloth and let rise in a warm, draft-free place until doubled in bulk, about 1 hour.

Butter two 1-pound loaf pans. Punch down the dough, divide it in half, and shape each half into a rectangular loaf. Place the loaves in the prepared pans, cover each loosely with a cloth, and let stand in a warm, draft-free place until the dough rises over the rims of the pans, about 30 minutes.

While the dough is rising, preheat the oven to 450°F Brush the tops of the loaves with the salt water and sprinkle oat flakes over the surface. Bake for 15 minutes, then reduce the oven temperature to 400°F and bake until the crust is dark brown and the bottom sounds hollow when tapped, another 30 to 40 minutes. Let the loaves cool slightly in the pans on racks, then remove and let them cool completely.

Makes 2 loaves.

F O U G A S S E A U X O L I V E S E T A N C H O I S
Olive and Anchovy Bread

This is the classic loaf of the Midi. It looks like a baseball glove. Indeed, there's a photo of Pablo Picasso, who adored this Mediterranean bread, seated at a table, with two *fougasses* in front of him that can be mistaken at first glance for his hands.

30 black olives, whole or halved, pits removed
10 anchovy fillets, with oil from tin
1 recipe baguette dough (page 120)

Preheat the oven to 450°F and place a heat-proof cup filled with water on the floor of the oven. Flour a baking sheet.

On a lightly floured surface, knead the olives and anchovies, including the oil, into the baguette dough, distributing them evenly. Divide the dough in half. Reflour the work surface and and roll one dough half into a rectangle about the size of this book. Lay your hand gently on the dough with your fingers apart. With the tip of a sharp knife, make four cuts in the dough between your fingers, cutting through to the work surface but not out to the edge. Make another *fougasse* in the same manner with the remaining dough.

Transfer the *fougasses* to the prepared baking sheet, cover with a light dish towel, and let rise until puffed, about 30 minutes. (If bubbles appear on the surface during this time, take a rolling pin and roll it very lightly over the dough to eliminate them.)

Roll down the *fougasses* very lightly one time. Bake in the oven for 30 minutes. Remove to a wire rack to cool.

Makes 2 fougasses.

B R I O C H E

To *"faire une brioche"* in French means to make an error. Musicians in the Paris opera used to fine each other for false notes, using the proceeds to buy brioches for rehearsal breaks.

Light, butter-yellow brioches came from the northeast of France where the best butter was made. In the Middle Ages, brioches were a market-day treat in dairy centers like Gournay and Gisors to the north of Paris, and Brie to the east. Their flavor depended on the "sweetness" of the butter and the character of the flour. Brioches were originally made with leaven but since the eighteenth century, they have been made with brewer's yeast. A good brioche should be moist and fluffy, with the flavor of the butter, but not the sour taste of the yeast. There are traditional recipes for princely brioches and common brioches; the more princely the brioche, the more butter and eggs it contains. Butter can make up half the weight.

In the nineteenth century, a baker named Lion, of the Rue de la Lune in Paris, reputedly made an excellent brioche by adding plum alcohol to the dough. He died late one night by his oven, the result of a cut he suffered from a broken bottle of wine. The story is still repeated by bakers for the warning it holds about the perils of lonely night work.

Brioche molds have flared, wavy sides, but brioches can also be baked in ring molds or bread tins. A large catering-size tin with one end removed is used by *boulangers* to make a brioche that resembles a chef's hat.

Brioches are the cornerstones of a bakery. *"Mauvaise brioche, mauvaise maison,"* say the French. If the brioche is poor, everything else will be, too.

2 teaspoons active dried yeast
2 tablespoons lukewarm water
3 teaspoons sugar
7 tablespoons unsalted butter, softened
1 cup plus 3 tablespoons all-purpose flour
3 large eggs
1 teaspoon salt
Melted butter for brushing

In a cup dissolve the yeast in the water with the sugar and let stand until foamy.

In a large bowl with an electric mixer, cream the butter until fluffy. In another bowl combine the flour with the eggs, one at a time, until thoroughly blended. Add the flour-egg mixture to the creamed butter and blend until combined. Turn off the mixer and pour in the proofed yeast. Blend until incorporated and add the salt. Knead until the dough is elastic and slightly sticky, but not so soft that it sticks to your fingers, about 10 minutes. Cover the bowl with a damp cloth and leave at room temperature overnight.

The next day, butter a 6-cup mold. Knead the dough for about 5 minutes by hand on a floured surface, or 2 minutes in a food processor, then transfer it to the prepared mold. Cover with a light dishcloth and let the dough rise until doubled in size, 2 to 3 hours, depending on the temperature in your kitchen.

While the dough is rising, preheat the oven to 450°F. Place the mold in the middle of the oven, reduce the oven temperature to 350°F, and bake for 20 minutes. (The deeper the mold, the longer the baking time.) The brioche is ready when it has a nice brown crust on top and the sides have come away slightly from the sides of the mold. If you slide a knife in, it should come out dry.

Remove to a wire rack to cool. While still warm, brush the top with melted butter.

Makes 1 brioche.

KUGELHOPF

This kind of brioche, with raisins in the dough and almond flakes on the crust, is a speciality of the Alsace region, near the German border. It's usually baked in a different mold, with a conical ring shape, and turned over for serving.

1 recipe brioche *dough (see page 132)*
¼ cup unblanched almond flakes
¾ cup raisins
Melted butter for brushing
Confectioners' sugar for sprinkling

Make the brioche dough, covering it and letting it rise at room temperature overnight.

Butter a *Kugelhopf* mold or a 6-cup ring mold and sprinkle the mold with the flaked almonds, covering the bottom and sides. Knead the raisins into the dough, distributing them evenly, then put the dough in the prepared mold. Cover and let the dough rise until it reaches the top of the mold, about 2 hours.

While the dough is rising, preheat the oven to 450°F. Place the mold in the middle of the oven, reduce the temperature to 400°F, and bake the *Kugelhopf* until it's browned on top and the sides have pulled away slightly from the mold, about 20 minutes. Brush the top with melted butter while still in the mold. Remove to a wire rack to cool. When cooled, dust the top with confectioners' sugar.

Makes one Kugelhopf.

PAIN PERDU
French Toast

Thanks to the system of staggered closing days, bread is always available fresh virtually everywhere in France. The French wouldn't think of eating it otherwise, leaving the problem of what to do with any bread left over from the day before. This is an old recipe for *pain perdu,* which means "lost bread."

1 loaf old, hard bread or brioche *(see page 132)*
1 large egg
1 ¼ cups milk
½ teaspoon orange-flower water (available in drugstores)
2 pinches of sugar
Pinch of salt
Plain, fresh bread crumbs for coating
Butter for cooking the bread

Cut the bread or brioche into thick slices. In a wide shallow bowl, beat the egg lightly.

In a saucepan heat the milk until hot, then add the orange-flower water, sugar, and salt. Dip the bread slices, one at a time, in the warm milk mixture and let the excess drip off. Dip the slices in the egg and let the excess drip off. Coat the dipped slices in the bread crumbs.

In a large skillet, melt a knob of butter until it has finished sizzling. Put the bread slices in the skillet and cook over medium heat until browned lightly. Turn and brown the other side. Sprinkle with sugar and serve hot.

VIENNOISERIE AND FLAKY PASTRIES

Here are the popular wares of a French bakery: *pains au lait* and *pains aux raisins,* and of course croissants. They are often known as *viennoiserie,* and you'll find them fresh in the morning waiting with baguettes and brioches. In the afternoons, *pains chocolat* and apple turnovers made with flaky pastry will be brought out, along with cookies called *palmiers,* and perhaps specialities like the *sacristain,* the *jesuit,* and the seasonal *galette des rois.*

PAINS AU LAIT
Viennese Buns

These were introduced in Paris by the Prussian entrepreneur Zang, who opened a bakery on the Rue de Richelieu and sold Viennese bread and cakes made with brewer's yeast.

5 tablespoons unsalted butter
1 ½ cups milk
2 ½ tablespoons active dry yeast
4 ½ cups plus 3 tablespoons all-purpose flour
¼ cup plus 2 teaspoons of sugar
3 large eggs
1 large egg, lightly beaten
Pearl sugar (decorative cubes, ⅛" square)

In a saucepan heat the butter in the milk over moderate heat, without boiling, until the butter is melted. Pour a small amount of the warm milk mixture into a large bowl, add the yeast, and let it dissolve until foamy. Add the remaining milk mixture. Beat in the flour, sugar, and eggs, one at a time. On a floured work surface, knead the dough until it is elastic, about 20 minutes. Cover the dough with a dishcloth and let it rise at room temperature until it has doubled in bulk, about 4 hours, depending on the temperature in your kitchen.

Butter and flour a baking sheet. Work the dough again, just for a few minutes. Form the dough into 20 ovals, each about 1 ½ inches long, and arrange them on the prepared baking sheet, leaving about 2 inches in between. Cover and allow to rise until not quite double in size, about 1 hour.

While the ovals are rising, preheat the oven to 425°F. Brush the ovals with the beaten egg, sprinkle the tops with

Miniature croissants and *pains chocolat* are a novelty
no less tempting than large ones. These are the staple *pâtisseries*.
The slices of *croquet*—a sweet loaf with almonds and hazelnuts—are another innovation.

pearl sugar, and bake them in the middle of the oven until browned, 5 to 10 minutes. Remove to a wire rack to cool.

Makes 20 small buns.

PAINS AUX RAISINS
Viennese Raisin Buns

These are the same buns baked in a flat, spiral shape, with raisins and a little dab of *crème pâtissière,* the genial pastry cream that turns simple buns into *pâtisserie.*

1 recipe Pains au lait *dough (see page 135)*
Crème pâtissière *(see page 157)*
½ cup raisins
1 large egg, lightly beaten

Prepare dough for *pains au lait,* covering it and letting it rise until it has doubled in bulk. Butter and flour a baking sheet.

On a lightly floured surface, knead the dough, then roll it into a rectangle about a ½ inch thick. Spread the crème pâtissière evenly over the dough, leaving a ½-inch border on all sides. Sprinkle the raisins over the cream, distributing them evenly.

Starting with a long side, roll the rectangle up jelly-roll fashion, but not tightly, pressing the seam gently closed. Place the roll, seam side down, on the work surface. With a sharp knife, cut the roll into ¾-inch slices. Lay the slices flat on the prepared baking sheet, leaving about 2 inches in between. Cover with a cloth and let rise for about an hour.

While the slices are rising, preheat the oven to 425°F. Brush the slices carefully with the beaten egg and bake in the middle of the oven until lightly browned, 5 to 10 minutes. Allow to cool under a cloth on a wire rack.

Makes about 20 buns.

CROISSANTS

Sometimes given a religious significance, the shape of croissants is owed to a military victory. Croissants originated in Budapest during the siege of 1686. When the Turks tried to tunnel under the city, bakers working at night heard them and raised the alarm. After the Turks had been repelled and the siege ended, bakers celebrated by making cakes in the shape of a crescent, emblem of the Ottoman empire.

That's how Alfred Grottshalk explained it in 1938 in the first edition of *Larousse Gastronomique*. Ten years later, in the second edition, he decided that the shape owed its origin to the siege of Vienna by Turkish forces. It's certain, at any rate, that croissants came to Paris from Vienna. They were originally Viennese breakfast buns (see the recipe on page 135) shaped in a crescent, and they were made popular by the Austrian princess Marie-Antoinette, who married Louis XVI and went on to make herself unpopular with an unfortunate remark about cakes.

The croissant made with flaky pastry was a French innovation of the 1920s. An enterprising Parisian baker—we don't know who—tried *feuilletée* techniques with a Viennese yeast-and-milk dough. Less butter is used than for a flaky pastry, and no salt. When they're good, they're irresistible, dunked in black coffee and eaten sopping wet. But they can leave a sour knot in the stomach if they haven't risen properly, somewhere not too warm, for the right length of time. In *boulangeries*, if they aren't designated *au beurre*, they're made with that dreadful French invention, margarine, and leave a dry taste in the mouth.

As for all doughs containing butter, it's important to work in a cool part of the kitchen, on a cool surface. That's why a marble *tour*, or worktop, is used by *patissiers*. In large *laboratoires*, the *tourier*—someone with quick but cool hands—does all the mixing. Work briskly, or the dough will become sticky and the butter will ooze. Put it back in the refrigerator if you feel this happening. Use a heavy rolling pin; less effort is needed, and both you and the dough will be less tired.

2 tablespoons brewer's yeast (available
in health-food stores)
About 3 tablespoons lukewarm water
3 ½ cups plus 1 tablespoon unbleached all-purpose flour
4 teaspoons sugar
1 teaspoon salt
1 cup plus 2 tablespoons milk
1 ¼ cups plus 1 tablespoon unsalted butter
1 large egg, lightly beaten

In a cup dissolve the yeast in the lukewarm water. In a large bowl, put the flour, sugar, and salt, and make a "well" in the middle. Pour the milk into the well and add a knob of butter. Add the proofed yeast and, working from the sides, incorporate the flour into the liquid until a dough forms that is homogeneous and no longer sticks to your hands. Cover the dough with a clean cloth and let it rise in a warm, draft-free place until it has doubled in bulk, about 1 hour.

Punch down the dough, knead it again briefly, and transfer it to a plate. Cover the dough with a damp cloth, then refrigerate until it's completely chilled, about 2 hours.

On a floured work surface roll out the dough into a rectangle 8 × 12 inches and ½ inch thick. In its wrapper or in a plastic bag, pound the remaining butter with a rolling pin to flatten it into a rectangle about two-thirds the size of the rectangle of dough.

Place the butter in the middle of the rectangle of dough. Fold both sides of the dough over the butter until they meet in the middle; fold the top and bottom edges until they meet in the middle, forming a "package." (The butter must be covered completely and the sides of the pastry unbroken.)

Flour the rolling pin and the work surface. Turn the dough over and position it so that a small side faces you, with the seam underneath. Rolling away from you, roll the dough into a rectangle 8 × 24 inches. Fold the dough into thirds, folding the top third over to the center and the bottom third up to cover the top, making an envelope.

Flour the work surface again. Roll the dough as directed above into a rectangle 8 × 24 inches. Fold the dough into thirds, as directed above. (This makes two complete "turns" of the dough.) Wrap the envelope in a dishcloth and chill it in the refrigerator for 20 minutes.

Roll out the dough and fold it into thirds two more times, for a total of four complete turns. (Always start with a short end facing you. If the dough becomes too soft to work, refrigerate it again.)

On a floured surface roll out the dough into a rectangle 12 × 36 inches. With a long, sharp knife, cut the dough in half lengthwise. Now cut each length of dough into triangles with bases of about 8 inches. (Cut squares of 6 inches, then cut them in half diagonally.)

To make croissants, start with the wide end of each triangle and loosely roll it up to form a cylinder. Stick the point down with a dab of water. Pull the ends around to form a crescent (see the photo on page 46). Repeat.

Transfer the crescents to a baking sheet, leaving at least 2 inches in between. Brush the crescents with the beaten egg, being careful not to drip any on the baking sheet. Let rise in a warm, draft-free place until doubled in size, about 2 hours, depending on the temperature in your kitchen.

Preheat the oven to 400°F. Brush the crescents again with egg, taking care not to let any drip, and bake them until golden brown, about 15 minutes. Transfer to racks to cool.

Makes about 15 croissants.

PAINS CHOCOLAT
Chocolate Puffs

Naturally, bakers in France have not been able to resist the challenge of improving on the croissant. Savory croissants made with cheese and ham are perhaps the only viable French fast food. Fancy croissants are made with flaked almonds and *crème d'amande* (see page 146), and powdered with confectioners' sugar before they're rolled and baked. The *pain chocolat* is made in a different shape but with the same pastry.

1 recipe croissant *pastry (see page 139)*
8 ounces bittersweet chocolate, cut into 2-inch fingers
1 large egg, lightly beaten

Butter and flour two baking sheets. On a lightly floured surface, roll the finished pastry into a rectangle 36 × 12 inches, as for croissants. Cut into bands 3 inches wide. Cut the bands into 4-inch lengths, making thirty-six 3 × 4-inch rectangles.

Place a finger of chocolate in the middle of each rectangle. Brush the edges of the pastry with the egg, then fold the pastry in half lengthwise over the chocolate. Transfer the pastries to the prepared baking sheets, leaving 3 inches in between, and let the pastries rise covered until nearly doubled in bulk, about 2 hours.

Preheat the oven to 400° F. Brush the tops of the pastries with egg and bake in the middle of the oven until browned, 20 to 30 minutes.

Makes 36 puffs.

PATE FEUILLETÉE
Flaky Pastry

To make the rest of the pastries in this section, you will need to make a puff or flaky pastry, a *pâte feuilletée*, which means "interleaved." The Romans baked it leaf by leaf. Renaissance chefs found a more efficient way, sandwiching the dough between layers of butter, a method French bakers perfected by using the best butter. Although this pastry is renowned as difficult to master, *boulangers* insist there's really nothing to it. As with croissants, it helps to keep the dough and butter cool. Work in a cool place and return the pastry to the refrigerator if it becomes too sticky.

Use a heavy rolling pin.

This pastry is also used for *vol-au-vents* and other savories, but the privilege of baking these belongs to *charcutiers*.

3 ½ cups plus 1 tablespoon unbleached all-purpose flour
1½ teaspoons salt or less, as desired
2 cups plus 3 tablespoons
unsalted butter
1 cup cold water

On a work surface, place the flour and make a "well" in the center. Add the salt and a scant ¼ cup (½ stick) butter cut in bits. With your fingertips, work the butter into the flour until the mixture has the texture of coarse crumbs. Add the water, a little at a time, incorporating it into the flour to form a soft, homogeneous dough. (The amount of water needed depends on the quality of the flour.) Form the dough into a ball and with a sharp knife cut a cross on top. Put the dough in a plastic bag and chill in the refrigerator for 30 minutes.

Lightly flour the work surface. Roll the dough into a rectangle 8 × 12 inches and ½ inch thick. In its wrapper or in a plastic bag, pound the butter with a rolling pin to flatten it into a rectangle two-thirds the size of the dough. (Work quickly so the butter stays cold.) Place the butter in the middle of the rectangle of dough. Fold both sides of the dough to meet at the center; fold the top and bottom edges of the dough to cover the butter, making a "package." (The butter must be entirely covered and the sides of dough not torn.) Cover with a cloth and chill in the refrigerator for 10 minutes.

Flour the rolling pin and the work surface again. Seam side down and with a short side towards you, roll the dough into a rectangle 8 × 24 inches. (Roll away from you, trying not to break the edges.) Fold the dough into thirds, folding the top third down to the center and the bottom third over to the top, making an envelope.

Flour the work surface again. With a short side facing you, roll the dough as directed above into a rectangle 8 × 24 inches. Fold the dough into thirds to form an envelope as directed above. (This makes two complete "turns" of the dough. Wrap the envelope in a cloth and chill it for 20 minutes.

Roll out the dough and fold it into thirds four more times, making a total of six complete turns. Make sure to chill the envelope after every two turns. Six turns produces classic *pâte feuilletée*.

After four turns, you can leave the pastry in the refrigerator or freeze it for up to three months before baking, wrapping it first in plastic wrap and then in aluminum foil. Make the last two turns before baking.

C H A U S S O N S   A U   P O M M E
Apple Turnovers

½ pound Golden Delicious apples
1 recipe pâte feuilletée *(see page 141)*
2 tablespoons sugar
1 large egg, lightly beaten

Preheat the oven to 400°F. Butter and flour a baking sheet. Peel, core, and quarter the apples, and cook with the sugar in a saucepan over low heat until a soft puree. On a lightly floured surface, roll the pastry into a ¼-inch-thick rectangle. Using a dessert plate as a guide, with the tip of a sharp knife cut six disks from the dough. In the middle of each disk spoon a rounded tablespoon of the pureed apple. For each turnover fold the pastry in half over the filling and press the edges together with a fork. Transfer the filled pastry to the prepared baking sheet and brush the tops with the egg. Bake them in the middle of the oven until golden and puffed, about 30 minutes. Allow to cool on a wire rack.

Makes 6 large turnovers.

PALMIERS
Flaky Pastry Cookies

*B*oulangers assemble these cookies from scraps of flaky pastry left over from cutting out rounds, but we've prepared a fresh *pâte feuilletée* for our *palmiers*. They are flat and wide, fanning out up to 9 inches in some *boulangeries*. The shape and the veined surface resemble those of a palm leaf, which gives them their name.

1 recipe pâte feuilletée *(see page 141)*
6 tablespoons confectioners' sugar

Preheat the oven to 400°F. Line a baking sheet with parchment paper.

Working in a cool part of the kitchen, dust your work surface with confectioners' sugar instead of flour before making

the last two turns of the pastry. Roll the flaky pastry into a ¼-inch-thick rectangle. Starting at the short ends roll up the pastry loosely, in jelly-roll fashion, from both ends so that the two rolls meet in the center.

With a sharp knife, cut this double roll into ½-inch slices. Dust the slices with confectioners' sugar and lay them flat on the prepared baking sheet, leaving about 2 inches in between each cookie. Bake in the middle of the oven until caramelized on the bottom and crisp, about 10 minutes. Turn the cookies over and bake until crisp and browned, another 10 to 15 minutes. Transfer to a wire rack to cool.

Makes 12 cookies.

SACRISTAINS
Flaky Pastry Sticks

1 recipe pâte feuilletée *(see page 141)*
1 cup firmly packed brown sugar
1 large egg, lightly beaten
1 cup ground almonds

Preheat the oven to 400°F. Line a baking sheet with parchment paper.

Working in a cool part of the kitchen, dust your work surface with the brown sugar instead of flour before making the last two turns of the flaky pastry. Roll out the pastry to a ¼-inch-thick rectangle. With a sharp knife, cut the pastry lengthwise into long, narrow strips about ¾ inch wide and 9 to 12 inches long.

Brush the strips with the beaten egg, then sprinkle the almonds over them. Holding one end, twist the other end of the strip over several times, ensuring that the twists are spaced evenly along the length. Transfer the strips to the prepared baking sheet, reduce the oven temperature to 350°F, and bake until lightly colored, about 30 minutes. Let the puff pastry sticks cool on a wire rack.

Makes about 15 sticks.

GALETTE DES ROIS
Epiphany Cake

The *galette des rois* is a traditional speciality of *boulangers*. Every January at Epiphany, which marks the arrival of the Three Wise Men with gifts for the baby Jesus, *boulangers* bake these large round *pâte feuilletées* filled with almond cream and encircled by a paper crown. Somewhere inside the *galette* is a charm—a silver coin or porcelain figurine, or just a dried bean in poorer versions—and the person whose portion contains the charm may wear the crown.

The tradition of nominating a mock king, and eating his *galette*, predates the Christian era, however. By medieval times, the whole household was turned upside down on the day of the Magi. Sons feasted at their father's expense, "learning luxury and larceny at the same time," according to one account. Portions of the *galette* were given to the poor and a toast was raised: "Praise the king, this he has earned / He's drunk his full, now it's our turn!"

At Epiphany, *boulangers* prepared *galettes* and gave them away to customers who, during the year, had bought their bread. The guild of *boulangers* presented one to the king. But *boulangers*—one of whom had already died at the hands of the mob—prudently ceased this custom when there was no longer a king to eat it. The *galette* then became the subject of a Revolutionary edict forbidding those of "liberticide" intentions from partaking of a cake that celebrated "the shadow of tyrants." The next year, *boulangers* produced *galettes de la*

Jean Jeudon, master baker at Ganachaud, Paris, removing a batch of *galettes des rois*. These flaky pastry cakes filled with almond cream used to be given away by bakers at Epiphany.

liberté, not with a crown but a Phrygian bonnet, the height of Jacobin chic, drawn by knifepoint on the top crust.

The *galette des rois* came back with the Restoration. Every January the windows of *boulangeries* are filled with them. *Boulangers* still gave them away to their customers until the First World War, and the guild still bakes a huge one for the mayor of Paris. Now they are bought by all, for the pleasure of the butter-rich pastry stuffed with almond cream and the ritual of the crown. The game of devouring slices to find the charm hidden inside is a fond memory of every French childhood.

The commercial zeal of *boulangers* helped to keep the tradition alive, but there was also the heretical pleasure of a mock coronation in a country that dispensed so abruptly with its king. The *galette des rois* is a large cake, to be shared by several people, but supermarkets now sell small and even individual galettes. In our self-obsessed consumer democracy it seems appropriate, though forlorn, that you should be able to elect yourself king.

1 recipe pâte feuilletée *(see page 141)*

FOR THE CRÈME D'AMANDE *FILLING:*

1 cup plus 3 tablespoons unsalted butter, softened
1 ¼ cups sugar
3 large eggs
1 cup plus 3 tablespoons ground almonds
⅓ cup unbleached all-purpose flour
Pinch of salt
5 drops pure almond extract
A charm
1 large egg, lightly beaten

Have ready the *pâte feuilletée.*

Make the *crème d'amande:* In the bowl of an electric mixer, cream the butter until fluffy. Add the sugar and eggs and blend until combined. Add the almonds, flour, and salt and blend until combined. Stir in the almond extract.

Makes enough for two cakes.

Preheat the oven to 400° F. Butter a baking sheet. On a lightly floured surface, roll the flaky pastry into a ⅛-inch-thick rectangle. Using a dinner plate as your guide, with the tip of a sharp knife cut out two circles of dough 10 to 12 inches in diameter. Transfer one of the rounds to the prepared baking sheet. Without puncturing the pastry, lay the charm in the round.

Spread the *crème d'amande* over the bottom round in an even layer, leaving a ½-inch border all around. Brush the border with the egg wash. Cover with the second pastry round and seal the edges together by pressing them with the tines of a fork. Pressing lightly, use the tines of the fork to make a wavy or zig-zag pattern on top. Brush the top with more egg wash. Bake in the middle of the oven until golden in color and lightly puffed, about 30 minutes.

Makes 1 cake.

TARTS

The French don't cover their fruit pies, and they call them *tartes*. These are the simplest of all *pâtisseries*. In the Middle Ages, they were just bread dough laden with fruit. Richer, more festive pastries like the sweet, crumbly shortcrust became common with the availability of good butter.

A *tarte* should be thin, no more than an inch deep, to keep the base from getting soggy from too much fruit juice. Any fruit that is fresh and in season will do. Sometimes custards are added to the apricot or cherry tarts from Alsace and Limousin, or a *crème pâtissière*.

Tarts were often prepared at home and brought to the *boulanger* to be cooked in the dying fires of the oven. In Zola's novel, *Le Ventre de Paris,* a denizen of nineteenth-century Paris brings a pear tart to the local *boulanger* and gossips with his wife as she waits for it to cook. The tradition has since died out, but tarts are still prepared and baked by *boulangers* for sale.

PATE BRISÉE
Shortcrust Pastry

This recipe for *pâte brisée,* the basic pastry for tarts, employs a mix of cake and all-purpose flour that simulates the flour in France, which is softer than the regular unbleached all-purpose flour available in the United States.

½ cup plus 2 ¼ teaspoons cake flour
½ cup plus 2 ¼ teaspoons all-purpose flour
½ cup plus ¾ tablespoon unsalted butter
Small pinch of salt
3 tablespoons cold water

Mix the flours, butter, and salt in a bowl, breaking the butter into small chunks into the flour. Working quickly, dash the water into the pastry until it feels smooth and not sticky. (The less you handle this pastry, the more tender it

Jean-Luc Poujauran experiments with regional specialties like *gâteau basque*—a kind of shortcake—and pine nut tarts, a taste from the Middle Ages. *Sablées* are biscuits with raisins and orange peel.

will be.) Seal the dough in a plastic bag and place it in the refrigerator for an hour before using.

Makes enough pastry for one 12-inch crust.

T A R T E   A U X   A B R I C O T S
Apricot Tart

This recipe will do for a tart with any kind of fruit, and the success of a tart depends on the fruit. If apricots aren't in season, use a fruit that is. Fruits that are ripe but still firm and not too juicy make the best tarts. The pieces should be placed tightly together so they don't dry out, and with rounded sides down if they're halved so the juice doesn't run out, making the pastry soggy.

A fig tart is a speciality of Provence, where the best ones grow. It is made like this apricot tart, except that the figs are unpeeled and less sugar is needed. The figs are halved and laid open side up.

1 recipe pâte brisée *(see page 148)*
2 tablespoons sugar
1 ½ pounds fresh apricots

Preheat the oven to 350°F. Lightly butter a 9-inch tart pan.

On a lightly floured surface, roll out the shortcrust pastry ⅛ to ¼ inch thick. Line the prepared pan with the pastry, trim the edges, and prick the pastry gently with a fork in several places. Sprinkle two-thirds of the sugar over the pastry.

Halve the apricots and remove the pits. Working from the outside edge of the pan, place the apricot halves on the pastry, rounded side down, in a tight spiral pattern. Sprinkle the rest of the sugar over the fruit.

Bake the tart in the middle of the oven until the crust is dry and golden brown, up to 45 minutes. Remove from oven and allow to rest 5 minutes. Remove tart from mold to cool on a wire rack before serving.

Makes one 9-inch tart.

TARTE AU POIRE
Pear Tart

Because of their long season, pears and apples are pop-ular for tarts. There is often a pear tart in the window of a French bakery. This one, with *crème pâtissière* added, was a speciality of La Varenne, who called it a *paste au poyres* in his seventeenth-century cookbook.

1 recipe pâte brisée (see page 148)
2 tablespoons sugar
1 pound fresh pears, not too juicy
1 recipe crème pâtissière (see page 157)
2 tablespoons blanched almonds flakes

Preheat the oven to 350°F. Lightly butter a 12-inch tart pan.

On a lightly floured surface, roll out the shortcrust pastry ⅛ to ¼ inch thick. Line the prepared pan with the pastry, trim the edges, and prick the pastry gently with a fork in several places. Sprinkle the sugar over the pastry.

Peel, seed, and halve the pears. Set them close together, rounded sides up. Bake the tart in the middle of the oven until the crust is dry and golden brown, up to 45 minutes. Allow to rest 5 minutes before removing from the pan to cool on a wire rack. When cool, pour a ½-inch layer of *crème pâtissière* around the pears and serve.

Makes one 12-inch tart.

TARTE AUX PIGNONS
Pine Nut Tart

Like the lemon tart that follows, the pine nut tart is many centuries old. The simplicity and delicate flavors of such tarts have brought them back into favor with bakers like Jean-Luc Poujauran.

1 recipe pâte brisée (see page 148)
¼ cup honey
¼ cup heavy cream
½ cup plus 2 tablespoons pine nuts

Preheat the oven to 350°F. Lightly butter a 9-inch tart pan.

On a lightly floured surface, roll out the shortcrust pastry ⅛ to ¼ inch thick. Line the prepared pan with the pastry, trim the edges, and prick the pastry gently with a fork in several places.

In a saucepan warm the honey slowly over moderate heat and stir in the cream; heat just until warm. Spread a ½-inch layer of the honey-and-cream mixture over the pastry. Pack the pine nuts tightly together over the honey-and-cream mixture, and bake the tart in the middle of the oven until the pastry is lightly colored, 15 to 20 minutes. Remove from oven and allow to rest 5 minutes. Remove from mold to cool on a wire rack before serving.

Makes one 9-inch tart or 3 small tartellettes.

TARTE AU CITRON
Lemon Tart

1 recipe pâte brisée (see page 148)
¾ cup sugar
2 large eggs
5 tablespoons unsalted butter
Juice of 2 lemons
Zest of 1 lemon, finely grated
Thin lemon slices for decoration

Preheat the oven to 325°F. Lightly butter a 12-inch tart pan. On a lightly floured surface, roll out the shortcrust pastry ⅛ to ¼ inch thick. Line the prepared pan with the pastry, trim the edges, and prick the pastry gently with a fork in several places.

In a bowl, using an electric mixer, beat the sugar and eggs together. In a saucepan, melt the butter over moderate heat and stir in the lemon juice and zest. Add to the egg-and-sugar mixture and combine well. Pour the filling into the pastry.

Bake the tart in the middle of the oven until the crust is light brown, about 30 minutes. Allow to rest for 5 minutes before removing from the mold. Cool on a wire rack, then refrigerate. Decorate the top of the tart with twists of sliced lemon.

Makes one 12-inch tart.

TARTE TATIN

The most famous of all French apple pies is the *tarte Tatin*, created by Stephanie Tatin, who, at the turn of the century, ran a hotel with her sister Caroline in the region of Sologne, in the town of Lamotte-Beuvron, opposite the railway station.

The construction of the railway had brought a new sort of clientele to the old coach house. One day, Stephanie was making an apple tart but, distracted by the gallantries of a guest, forgot to line the dish with pastry before putting in the apples. She put the pastry on top of the apples and cooked her tart upside down. Once it was turned over, the juices at the bottom had created a rich caramel top.

Like almost everything in *pâtisserie,* this reversal was not new. There were medieval recipes for upside-down

tarts, but the one prepared by the Tatin sisters was singled out for praise by Curnonsky in his epic work, *La France Gastronomique.* Curnonsky attributed the unique flavor of the *tarte des demoiselles* Tatin to the apples from the orchards of the marshy Sologne, and to the quantity of sugar and butter. He advised using as much sugar and butter, pound for pound, as apples.

The Hotel Tatin run by the sisters is still there. It has been taken over by Monsieur Caille and his wife. Monsieur Caille is a chef who cooks several *tarte Tatin* each week for guests who come from as far away as Japan and the United States to savor this unique French apple pie. If requested, he serves it with ice cream. Vanilla ice cream is the one people prefer, he explains. He places the scoops beside the portion of *tarte Tatin,* a little reluctantly.

It puzzles him that such a tart should require any enhancement. The best apples, the best butter—plenty of it— and the right amount of sugar: These are what makes a good *tarte Tatin.* The cooking times depend on the juiciness of the apples. More time is needed for apples with high water content. His secret is to pass the bottom of the baking dish over the heat briefly after the tart has cooked, to caramelize the sugary apple juice. He notices that some

A *tarte Tatin* baked by Gilles Caille, present owner of the Hotel Tatin,
on the stove the Tatin sisters used to bake their famous upside-down apple pie.

visitors like to place the vanilla ice cream on top of the tart, so that it melts. But he says nothing. "Everyone has their preference," he philosophizes.

———————

1 cup plus 2 tablespoons sugar
2 pounds apples, preferably Golden Delicious
½ cup plus ¾ tablespoon unsalted butter, cut into pieces
½ recipe pâte brisée *(see page 148)*

Preheat the oven to 350°F. Generously butter a 10-inch-wide, 3-inch-deep glass baking dish and sprinkle about a third of the sugar over the bottom. Peel, core, and quarter the apples. Pack the apple quarters tightly together in the baking dish. Dot the apples with the butter and a sprinkling of the remaining sugar. Bake in the middle of the oven for 25 minutes.

Just before the apples finish baking, on a lightly floured surface roll out the pastry ⅛ to ¼ inch thick. Place the pastry over the apples, and tuck it in at the sides of the dish. With the tip of a sharp knife, cut several steam vents in the pastry. Bake for 30 minutes.

Remove the dish from the oven and place on a hot heating element. Through the glass you will see the sugary juice start to caramelize. The tart is ready for inverting when a small amount of brownish syrup forms at the bottom of the dish. Take care not to let this caramel burn. Turn the tart upside down onto a plate and serve hot.

Makes one 10-inch tart.

———————

PATE SABLÉE
Sable Pastry

For certain kinds of tarts, a dry, biscuitlike pastry, also known as sugar pastry crust, is preferable. Tarts with berries are often made with this kind of pastry.

———————

½ cup plus 1½ tablespoons cake flour
½ cup plus 1½ tablespoons all-purpose flour
⅔ cup plus 2½ tablespoons granulated sugar
Pinch of salt
1 large egg
½ cup plus ¾ tablespoon unsalted butter, cut into bits
Zest of 1 lemon or ½ teaspoon vanilla sugar

———————

In a bowl, combine the flours, granulated sugar, salt, and egg. Work the pastry, adding the chunks of butter, lemon zest, or vanilla sugar. Shape the pastry into a ball, seal it in a plastic bag, and refrigerate for 1 hour.

Preheat the oven to 350°F. Lightly butter a 9-inch pie plate. Place the sable pastry directly in the pie plate, and with the heel of your hand spread it out to line the bottom and sides of the plate. Crimp the edge decoratively. Line the bottom of the shell with parchment paper, then cover with dried beans or pie weights. A sparse layer is enough to prevent the pastry from puffing up. Bake the empty shell until the pastry starts to pull away from the sides of the pan, 15 to 20 minutes. Remove the shell from the oven, let it cool thoroughly, and remove the paper and dried beans.

You must precook, or blind-bake, the pastry in this way for tarts with fragile fruits that shouldn't be cooked, like strawberries or raspberries. There is no need to precook the pastry if the fruit can be cooked, such as blueberries.

In addition to making tart shells, *pâte sablée* can be used for sweet cookies called *sablées*. Roll the pastry into a tube shape by hand, slice into thin rounds, and bake until brown, about 20 minutes.

Makes enough for one 12-inch crust.

TARTE AUX FRAISES
Strawberry Tart

1 recipe pâte sablée *(see page 152)*
1 recipe crème pâtissière *(recipe follows)*
2 pints fresh strawberries, hulled
Strawberry jelly for glazing

Blind-bake a sable pastry tart shell, let it cool down thoroughly, and remove from the pie plate. Cover the bottom of the shell with a ¼-inch layer of crème pâtissière. Allow to set in the refrigerator before arranging the strawberries on the pastry cream closely together.

Melt the strawberry jelly in a small saucepan or in a heat-proof cup set in a pan of hot water (known as a *bain-marie*). Allow the melted jelly to cool almost to the point of setting. Gently spoon a layer of melted jelly over the strawberries, glazing them. Place the tart in the refrigerator for an hour before serving.

Makes one 12-inch tart.

CRÈME PATISSIÈRE
Pastry Cream

2 cups milk
½ vanilla bean or 5 ounces bittersweet chocolate (more
than 50% cocoa) or zest of 1 lemon or 1 tablespoon
kirsch or Grand Marnier
6 large egg yolks
⅔ cup plus 5 tablespoons sugar
⅓ cup unbleached all-purpose flour

In a medium-size, heavy saucepan bring the milk to a boil with the desired flavoring (except kirsch or Grand Marnier). If using chocolate, it can be coarsely chopped or grated into the milk. Reduce the heat to moderate and let the milk simmer gently.

In a large bowl, using an electric mixer, beat the egg yolks with the sugar until very pale, almost white in color. Gradually beat in the flour. If using vanilla bean, remove it from the hot milk and pour the hot milk slowly and steadily over the egg mixture, beating until combined. Return the mixture to the saucepan and bring to a boil over moderate heat, whisking constantly. Continue to boil while whisking for a few minutes, until it thickens and is smooth in texture.

If you're using kirsch or Grand Marnier, stir it at this time into the pastry cream after it has cooled slightly. If you're not using the pastry cream immediately, rub some butter over the surface to prevent a skin forming.

Makes about 2½ cups, more than enough for recipes in this book. The rest can be frozen once it has cooled.

ÉCLAIRS

Simple and light, though made without yeast—just eggs, flour, and melted butter—the *pâte â choux* used for éclairs is one of the easiest of pastries to produce, yet it wasn't commonly made by *pâtissiers* until Carême gave a recipe in his *Pâtissier Royal* in 1815. Sometimes attributed to the chefs of Catherine de Medici, choux pastry was perhaps an invention of the Enlightment: *Éclair* means a flash of light, and the genius of the éclair is that it's essentially a way to eat the cream filling. Before latter-day enlightenment found a way to make synthetic cream from cornstarch and air, these choux buns were very much worth eating.

With the recipe for *crème pâtissière* described on page 157, we passed into the elevated realm of *pâtisserie*. The creation of creams with subtle flavors was one of the things that distinguished the *pâtissier* from the humble baker of bread and tarts. A contemporary of Carême, a certain Fauvel, created one of the first varieties of choux buns, filled with what he called *crème Chiboust*, the name of the *maison* in Paris where he worked. The recipe for the cream was Fauvel's secret. He called his choux buns *saint-honorés* in honor of the patron saint of French bakers. The airy, evanescent choux epitomized the ideal of all bakers—to produce something so light and delicious it just disappears.

Within no time there were as many recipes for cream fillings as there were bakers. And each had a name for his own sort of cream-filled choux bun: the *religieuse*, three buns with a fourth set on top, a shape that resembles a nun's hat; the *divorce*, a double éclair, one filled with coffee cream and the other with chocolate; choux buns with vanilla-flavored *crème pâtissière* called *carolines*; the *salammbô*, named after Flaubert's scandalous novel; and, of course, the éclair.

The Paris-Brest—a ring of choux pastry filled with egg cream and meringue—was named for a bicycle race from Paris to the port of Brest and back. A *pâtissier* named Durand, whose bakery was

"Gluttony is not a sin but a virtue," according to Saint Honoré, the patron saint of bakers. You'll see chocolate- and caramel-glazed éclairs to the right of the sign.

on the cyclists' route through the suburb of Maisons-Lafitte, created it in 1910, consecrating the excitement in a wheel-shaped cake. The race has been eclipsed by the Tour de France, but the great-grandson of the imaginative *pâtissier* is still there, in the same premises, baking Paris-Brests.

PATE A CHOUX
Choux Pastry

Carême added grated Parmesan and melted Gruyère to his *pâte à choux,* with a pinch of sugar to mask the sourness of the cheeses. Like the *pâte feuilletée,* this is a very versatile though much simpler pastry, which can also be used for savory *petit fours.*

7 tablespoons unsalted butter
1 cup water
2 teaspoons sugar
Pinch of salt
⅔ cup plus 2½ tablespoons unbleached all-purpose flour
4 large eggs

Preheat the oven to 425°F. Butter a baking sheet.

In a large saucepan, melt the butter with the water, sugar, and salt. Bring the mixture to a boil, remove from heat, and immediately dump all the flour into the saucepan at one time. Stir the mixture vigorously with a wooden spoon until it leaves the sides of the pan. Add the eggs one at a time, stirring vigorously. For plain choux buns, put golf ball-size lumps of pastry on the prepared baking tray and cook in the middle of the oven, reducing the temperature to 400°F after 10 minutes. They are ready when puffed and light brown, 15 to 20 minutes, depending on size.

Makes 20 to 25 buns.

CHOQUETTES
Choux Buns

1 recipe pâte à choux *(see this page)*
1 large egg yolk
Pearl sugar (decorative cubes, ⅛" square)

Preheat the oven to 425°F. Butter a baking sheet. Form the choux pastry into lumps the size of golf balls and arrange them on the prepared baking sheet 2 inches apart.

Beat the egg yolk until combined. With a pastry brush paint the tops of the buns with the yolk, taking care not to let any yolk drip onto the tray, as this would prevent the buns from rising. Sprinkle the tops of the buns generously with sugar.

Bake the buns in the middle of the oven for 10 minutes. Reduce the temperature to 400°F and bake until puffed and golden brown, 10 minutes longer. Transfer buns to a wire rack to cool completely.

Makes 20 to 25 buns.

ÉCLAIRS AU CHOCOLAT
Chocolate Éclairs

1 recipe pâte à choux *(see page 160)*
1 recipe crème pâtissière *(see page 157), flavored with chocolate*

FOR THE CHOCOLATE GLAZE:

3 ounces bittersweet chocolate
6 tablespoons (¾ stick) unsalted butter
3 large eggs, separated

Preheat the oven to 425°F. Butter a baking sheet.

Fill a pastry bag fitted with a no. 4 or no. 7 round tip with the choux pastry, and on the prepared baking sheet pipe out 3-inch lengths, leaving 1½ inches in between. Bake for 10 minutes, then reduce the temperature to 400°F and bake until puffed and golden, 20 minutes longer. Transfer the pastries to a wire rack and let cool completely. When cool, halve them horizontally with a serrated knife.

Fill the bottom halves of the éclairs with the chocolate crème pâtissière and gently replace the tops.

Make the chocolate glaze: In a medium-size heat-proof bowl set in a pan of simmering water, melt the chocolate with the butter.

In a medium-size bowl, beat the egg whites with an electric mixer until stiff peaks form. Remove the pan of chocolate butter from the heat and add the egg yolks, stirring well to combine. Fold in the stiffened egg whites.

With a pastry brush, paint the tops of the éclairs carefully with the chocolate glaze. Keep the pastries in a cool place to allow the glaze to harden.

Makes 20 to 25 small éclairs.

SALAMMBOS

1 recipe pâte à choux *(see page 160)*
1 recipe crème pâtissière *(see page 157), flavored with
kirsch or Grand Marnier*

FOR THE CARAMEL GLAZE:

*¾ cup sugar
Few drops fresh lemon juice
3 tablespoons water*

Preheat the oven to 425° F. Butter a baking sheet.

With a pastry bag fitted with a no. 4 round tip, pipe
lengths of choux pastry 1½ inches long onto the baking
sheet, 2 inches apart. Bake for 10 minutes, then reduce the
temperature to 400° F and bake until they have a dry, gold-
en color, about 15 minutes longer. Remove from the oven,
and after 5 minutes transfer to a wire rack to cool. With a
serrated knife, halve the pastries horizontally. Fill the
bottom half of each choux puff with the flavored *crème
pâtissière*.

Make the caramel glaze: In a small, heavy saucepan melt
the sugar over low heat, adding the lemon juice drop by
drop. Bring the sugar to a boil, reduce to moderate heat, and
add the water a tablespoon at a time, swirling the pan. Stir
the caramel; it should be light brown in color and still liquid. Allow to cool.

Carefully dip the top half of each puff pastry into the
caramel and arrange the tops on the filled bottom halves.

Makes 25 to 30 salammbôs.

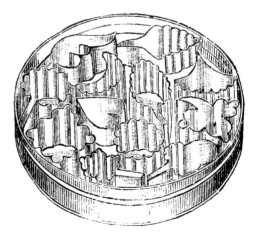

AMANDINES, BABAS, AND MORE

These are some of the favorite cakes sold in *boulangeries* and *pâtisseries:* simple sponge cakes like madeleines, and custard pies like the *far* and *clafouti* that originated in the Middle Ages, as well as macaroons, which date from the Renaissance, and meringues from the Restoration. And, from an old *pâtisserie* in Paris, the *baba au rhum.*

AMANDINES
Almond Tarts

Like the *far* and *clafouti* that follow, *amandines* can be cooked in pie dishes, but there is no need to line the dish with shortcrust pastry as you would for a tart.

1 cup plus 2 tablespoons sugar
2 large eggs
2 large eggs, separated
½ cup ground almonds plus ¾ tablespoon
sliced almonds
4 drops pure almond extract
1 teaspoon salt
Juice and zest of 1 lemon
⅔ cup plus 2½ tablespoons cake flour
2½ tablespoons potato or corn flour

Preheat the oven to 350° F. Butter a 9-inch tart pan.

In a large bowl, beat together the sugar, 2 eggs, and the 2 egg yolks. Stir in the ground almonds, almond extract, and salt. Add the lemon juice and zest. Gradually beat in the cake and potato flours.

In another bowl, with an electric mixer, beat the 2 egg whites until they form stiff peaks. Gently fold the beaten whites into the almond mixture.

Spread the batter in the prepared pan and sprinkle the almond slices over the surface. Bake in the middle of the oven until the tart is browned around the edges and the almonds on the top begin to brown, about 45 minutes. Transfer the tart to a wire rack to cool before serving.

Makes one 9-inch tart or 3 small tartelettes.

Custard tarts or *clafoutis:* plain, with candied fruits, and flavored with lemon.

FAR
Raisin Custard Cake

This can be made with raisins or other kinds of dried fruit, or with none at all, a *far naturel.*

---

5 large eggs, lightly beaten
2/3 cup plus 2 1/2 tablespoons cake flour
1/2 cup sugar
2 cups lukewarm milk
2/3 cup raisins

Preheat the oven to 350°F. Butter a deep 9-inch tart dish.

In a bowl stir together the eggs, flour, and sugar until combined. Stir the warm milk into the mixture, then transfer the batter to the prepared dish. Sprinkle the raisins over the batter. Bake the custard in the middle of the oven until puffed and brown on top and cooked through, 45 minutes to 1 hour. Let cool slightly in the dish and serve warm.

Makes one 9-inch cake.

CLAFOUTI
Baked Cherry Pancake

---

3 large eggs
6 teaspoons sugar, plus more for sprinkling
1/2 cup plus 1 tablespoon cake flour
Pinch of salt
1 1/4 cups cold milk
1 1/2 pounds firm fresh black cherries, stems and pits removed and halved, if large

Preheat the oven to 350°F. Butter a deep 9-inch tart dish.

In a bowl beat the eggs together with the sugar, flour, and salt. Beat in the milk gradually. The batter should be fluffy and lump free, like pancake batter.

Arrange the cherries close together over the bottom of the prepared dish and pour the batter over them. Sprinkle with sugar. Bake in the middle of the oven until a knife inserted in the center of the custard comes out dry, 30 to 40 minutes. The pancake will rise in the oven and fall at once when removed. Serve warm or at room temperature.

Makes one 9-inch pancake.

Macarons au Chocolat
Chocolate Macaroons

These simple sugar and almond cookies were beloved of Catherine de Medici, who introduced them to France. Later, *pâtissiers* sandwiched them together with a filling of *crème au beurre* and added flavorings, such as chocolate and coffee.

FOR THE CHOCOLATE MACAROONS:

4 large egg whites
1 ¼ cups granulated sugar
½ cup plus ¾ tablespoon ground almonds
¼ cup confectioners' sugar
2 tablespoons unsweetened cocoa powder
Pinch of salt

FOR THE CHOCOLATE BUTTERCREAM:

10½ tablespoons unsalted butter, softened
5 ounces bittersweet chocolate (more than 50% cocoa)
½ cup confectioners' sugar
2 tablespoons water
4 large egg yolks

Preheat oven to 350° F. Line a baking sheet with parchment paper.

Make the chocolate macaroons: In a large bowl, using an electric mixer, beat the egg whites until frothy. Gradually add ¼ cup of the granulated sugar and beat the whites until stiff peaks form. In another bowl combine the almonds with the remaining granulated sugar, the confectioners' sugar, cocoa powder, and salt. Gently fold in the egg whites.

With a regular teaspoon, place spoonfuls of the batter on the prepared baking sheet, leaving about 1 inch in between. Bake in the middle of the oven until the crust is dry, about 15 minutes. Sprinkle some water on the baking tray, under the parchment paper. (The humidity will help to detach the macaroons from the paper when they have cooled a little.) Remove to a wire rack to cool thoroughly.

Make the chocolate buttercream: In a small bowl, using an electric mixer, cream the butter while the macaroons are cooling. Melt the chocolate slowly in the top of a double boiler over simmering water or in a heat-proof cup set in a pan of hot water (*bain-marie*).

In a small saucepan, combine the sugar and water and bring gently to a boil. Simmer for 5 to 10 minutes. Test for readiness by dropping a teaspoon of the syrup in a glass of cold water. If a ball forms, the syrup is ready.

In a medium-size bowl, using an electric mixer, beat the egg yolks until light in color. With the mixer running, carefully pour in the hot sugar syrup and beat until combined. Add the melted chocolate and creamed butter and beat until fluffy and slightly shiny. Sandwich two cookies together with a dab of chocolate buttercream to form egg-shaped macaroons.

For coffee-flavored macaroons, use instant coffee instead of the chocolate. Dissolve in a little water for both the macaroon biscuit and the buttercream filling.

Makes about 30 small macaroons.

MERINGUES

4 large egg whites
1 ¼ cups sugar

Preheat the oven to 200° to 225° F. Butter and flour a baking sheet.

In a large bowl, using an electric mixer, beat the egg whites until they form soft peaks. Gradually add the sugar and continue beating the egg whites until stiff, glossy peaks form.

Drop teaspoonfuls (or tablespoonfuls for larger ones) of the meringue onto the prepared baking sheet, leaving 1 ½ to 2 inches in between. Bake in the middle of the oven until the meringues are dry, 1 to 1 ½ hours. Remove to a wire rack to cool.

Makes 20 to 40 meringues, depending on size.

BABAS AU RHUM
Rum Babas

The *baba* was named for Ali Baba, hero of the *Thousand and One Nights,* the favorite book of King Stanislas, the Polish king exiled in France. It was the King's baker, Stohrer, who invented it, and this is how they're made at the *pâtisserie* that still bears his name, where they were first sold more than two centuries ago.

5 tablespoons unsalted butter
2 packages active dried yeast
⅓ cup lukewarm water
4½ teaspoons sugar
2½ cups unbleached all-purpose flour
1½ teaspoons salt
3 large eggs

FOR THE RUM SOAK:

1 cup water
¾ cup sugar
¼ to ½ cup dark rum

FOR DECORATION:

Apricot jam, heated
Angelica
Glacéed cherries

In a small saucepan melt the butter and set it aside to cool. In a small bowl combine the yeast and water with a pinch of the sugar and let set until foamy, or proofed.

In a large bowl sift the flour, the remaining sugar, and the salt. Add the eggs and blend well with a wooden spoon or your hands. Add the proofed yeast and start kneading the dough by lifting, folding, and slapping it against the sides of the bowl for a few minutes. (The dough will be soft and very sticky.) Work in the melted butter, which must have cooled thoroughly, and continue to knead the dough until elastic.

Dust a bowl with flour and put the dough in it. Cover the bowl with a dampened cloth, and let it rise until doubled in bulk, 1 to 2 hours.

Preheat the oven to 400°F. Butter 12 baba molds or muffin tins measuring 2 inches deep and 2 inches in diameter. Using a tablespoon, fill each cup one-third full. Let the dough rise, uncovered, until it mushrooms above the rims of the molds, about 1 hour.

Place the molds in the upper third of the oven and bake 10 to 20 minutes, depending on the size of the molds. The babas are done when they are nicely brown on top and the sides have shrunk away from the sides of the cups. Unmold the babas onto a wire rack.

Make the rum soak: In a saucepan bring the water to a boil, add the sugar, and stir to dissolve. Remove the pan from the heat and let the syrup cool to lukewarm. Stir in the rum.

Arrange the still-warm babas in a dish, and spoon the rum soak over them. Let them stand for 30 minutes. Baste with the syrup in the dish.

For decoration: After the babas have soaked, drain the remaining syrup, if necessary, then brush the babas with the apricot jam to form a glaze. (This will keep the babas from drying out if they are to be kept for several days.) Lay the babas on their sides and decorate with pieces of angelica and glacéed cherries.

Makes 12 babas.

SAVARIN

At Stohrer, the babas are shaped like large, stubby mushrooms, and laid on their sides. They're made with cylindrical molds. The more familiar ring-shaped babas are in fact small savarins, a cake created a century later by Auguste Julien, a celebrated Parisian *pâtissier.*

The savarin is baked in a ring mold, using the same dough as a baba, with almond flakes for decoration. It's soaked in syrup made with kirsch rather than rum, and garnished with Chantilly cream. It was named after the author Brillat-Savarin, who had just published his much-talked-about *The Physiology of Taste,* which inquired, among other things, into the reason that cakes should be so irresistible.

1 recipe baba *dough (see page 168)*
2 tablespoons raisins
¼ cup blanched almond flakes

FOR THE KIRSCH SOAK:

2 cups water
1 ½ cups sugar
Kirsch to taste
Apricot jam, heated
Blanched almond flakes
Whipped cream, to taste

Have the baba dough ready. Butter a large ring mold and arrange the raisins and almond flakes over the bottom. After the first rising, put the dough into the prepared mold and let it rise, uncovered, until it reaches the top of the mold, about 1 hour.

Preheat the oven to 400°F. Bake the savarin until it begins to pull away from the sides of the mold, 30 to 35 minutes. Allow to cool for 5 minutes. Invert the savarin onto a dish and allow it to cool further until the mold feels loose. Remove the mold and cool the savarin completely.

Make the kirsch soak: In a saucepan bring the water to a boil, add the sugar, and stir to dissolve. Remove the pan from the heat and let the syrup cool to lukewarm. Stir in kirsch to your taste. Ladle the syrup gently over the savarin. Baste with the syrup in the dish. Brush with the heated apricot jam to glaze. Sprinkle with flaked almonds and fill the center with whipped cream.

Makes 1 savarin.

PAIN D'ÉPICE
Spice Cake

Pilgrims brought spices back to Europe from the Holy Land, where they had tasted them in cakes and buns. In convents and monasteries, spices were added to traditional honey cakes. By medieval times, spices had become a chic, metropolitan taste. They were sold for up to thirty times their original cost, but still there weren't enough spices available to satisfy demand. Cinnamon—the bark of a tree native to Sri Lanka and the Malabar coast of India— was more expensive than gold. It was used in Egypt for embalming, and in Europe for religious ceremonies. Quills of rolled cinnamon bark were the most profitable spice traded by the Dutch East India Company, until it was planted in the West Indies. And it was the European taste for cinnamon, nutmeg, and cloves that led to the inadvertent discovery of the Americas.

With the Renaissance, sugar overtook spices in popularity. And from the Americas, where they were discovered, chocolate and vanilla were soon the rage. But spice cakes remained popular, especially one made in Rheims and first sold in 1420 in honor of Charles VII, the *petit roi.* It was made with rye flour, dark honey, and cinnamon. Charles's mistress, Agnes Sorel, the *Dame de beauté,* never travelled without some. Thanks to her, spice cake from Rheims became celebrated throughout France, though it was baked elsewhere, too. A hundred miles farther east in Alsace, it was made with cinnamon and grains of anise, the recipe given here. Farther south in Dijon, the rye and honey were left to mature in wooden barrels for months. After baking, too, it improves with age.

1 cup plus 3 tablespoons rye flour
⅓ cup chopped unblanched almonds
½ cup plus 2¼ tablespoons honey
½ cup plus 2 tablespoons milk
*2 teaspoons green anise seeds (available in baking supply
stores) or ground anise*
1 teaspoon ground cinammon
2 teaspoons baking soda
2 large egg yolks

Preheat the oven to 350°F. Butter two 1-pound loaf pans.

In a large bowl combine the flour and almonds. In a saucepan heat the honey over moderate heat until melted; add the milk, anise seeds, and cinnamon and stir to combine. Remove the pan from the heat, pour a small amount of it into a cup, and to this add the baking soda. Let the remaining milk mixture cool, then add the egg yolks, one at a time. Add the milk-and-egg yolk mixture to the flour and almonds; add the dissolved baking soda, and mix the dough until it is no longer sticky.

Divide the dough between the two prepared loaf pans and bake until nicely browned on top, or until a knife inserted in the center comes out dry, 30 to 40 minutes. After 5 minutes, transfer the loaves to wire racks to cool.

Makes 2 cakes, best eaten after a day or two.

MADELEINES

The best madeleines, according to Alexandre Dumas, came from the village of Commercy, in Alsace. Some say these simple little sponge cakes were first baked by a certain Madeleine Paumier, a cook in the local château. Dumas attributed them to King Stanislas, the Polish king whose court-in-exile at Lunéville was not far from Commercy. The king—eventually tiring of babas—reputedly became fond of the wares of a pretty local girl named Madeleine.

However, the town of Illiers, to the south of Paris, is also renowned for its madeleines. The shell-like molds used to bake them were associated with Saint James, whose emblem was a shell. Pilgrims on their way to the shrine of Santiago (St. James) de Compostela in Spain would have been eager customers for shell-shaped cakes along the route. And even before the Christian era, a shell would have made a convenient baking mold.

There is something intemporal about madeleines, perhaps because of their long but obscure history. Every year, a private contest is held among *pâtissiers* to bake madeleines so light they won't come down if you throw them in the air.

French children are known to adore madeleines, and all cakes reawaken the delight of the child in us. If tastes endure for generations, it's perhaps because childhood memories are the deepest. Taste and smell are primordial senses. The recollection of a taste will last a lifetime, and during that lifetime, it will be passed on to another generation. Marcel Proust began his epic *Remembrance of Things Past* with the childhood memories that "sprang into being" from a cup of tea when, out of habit, he dunked a madeleine in it. He wrote: "Taste and smell alone, more fragile but more enduring, more unsubstantial, more persistent, more faithful, remain poised a long time, like souls, remembering, waiting, hoping, amid the ruins of all the rest."

Nowadays, madeleines are usually made with vanilla. This recipe uses the old European flavoring of orange flowers.

---

3 large eggs, separated
¼ cup plus 2 teaspoons unsalted butter
¾ cup plus 2 tablespoons cake flour
¾ cup sugar
½ teaspoon orange-flower water
(available in drugstores)
Zest of ½ lemon

Preheat the oven to 350° F. Butter and flour madeleine molds, or small muffin molds.

In a large bowl, using an electric mixer, beat the egg whites until they form stiff peaks. In a saucepan melt the butter over moderate heat, then remove the pan from the heat. Stir the flour and sugar into the butter until combined. Stir in the orange-flower water, lemon zest, and egg yolks; combine well. Fold the yolk mixture gently but thoroughly into the beaten egg whites.

Fill each mold about three-quarters full with batter. Bake the cakes on the lowest shelf of the oven, until they are a light golden color, 20 to 30 minutes. Transfer the cakes to a wire rack to cool completely.

Makes 26 madeleines.

SOME *PÂTISSERIES* AND *BOULANGERIES*

PÂTISSERIES

Brocco
180 Rue du Temple, 75003 Paris

Duchesne
112 Rue Saint Dominique, 75007 Paris

Durand
9 Avenue Longueil, 78600 Maisons-Lafitte

Martine Carton
6 Rue de Buci, 75006 Paris

Peltier
66 Rue de Sevres, 75007 Paris

Stohrer
51 Rue Montorgueil, 75002 Paris

BOULANGERIES

Béchu
118 Avenue Victor Hugo, 75016 Paris

Boisguerin
9 Rue Louise Michel, 94600 Choisy Le Roi

A La Flûte Gana
226 Rue des Pyrénées, 75020 Paris

Ganachaud
150 Rue de Menilmontant, 75020 Paris

Le Moulin de la Vierge
82 Rue Daguerre, 75014 Paris
105 Rue Vercingetorix, 75014 Paris
166 Avenue de Suffren, 75015 Paris

Lionel Poilâne
49 Boulevard de Grenelle, 75015 Paris
8 Rue du Cherche Midi, 75006 Paris

Max Poilâne
87 Rue Brancion, 75015 Paris

Jean-Luc Poujauran
20 Rue Jean Nicot, 75007 Paris

CHRONOLOGICAL BIBLIOGRAPHY

La Varenne. *Le Patissier François.* Elsevier, 1655.

Parmentier. *Le parfait boulanger.* Imprimerie Royale, 1778.

Carême, Marie-Antonin. *Le Pâtissier Royale Parisien,* 1815.

————. *Le Pâtissier Pittoresque,* 1815.

Brillat-Savarin. *Le Physiologie du gout,* 1826.

Dumas, Alexandre. *Grand Dictionnaire de Cuisine,* 1873.

Urbain-Dubois. *Grand Livre des Pâtissiers et Confisiers,* 1883.

Lacam, Pierre. *Memorial historique de la pâtisserie,* 1888.

Sebillot, Paul. *Traditions et superstitions de la boulangerie,* 1891.

Morel, Ambroise. *Histoire de la boulangerie.* Syndic Patronale, 1924.

Calvel, Raymond. *La boulangerie moderne.* Eyrolles, 1952.

David, Elizabeth. *English Bread & Yeast Cookery.* Allen Lane, 1977.

Thouvenot, Claude. *Le pain d'autrefois.* André Leson, 1977.

Poilâne, Lionel. *Guide de l'amateur du pain.* Laffont, 1981.

————. *Faire son pain.* Dessain et Tolra, 1982.

Bouyer, Christian. *Folklore du boulanger.* Maisonneuve & Larose, 1984.

INDEX

Numbers in *italics* indicate illustrations

affaires
    defined, 48
Alexander the Great, 52
Ali Baba, 167
almond
    cream *(crème d'amande)*, 64, 72, 78, 140, 144, 146–47
    tart, 8, 163
amandine, 8, 163
américaines, 12
Amon, Gilles *(pâtissier)*, 26, 36
Amon, Roland *(boulanger)*, 12, 13, 15, 22, 24–30, *31*, 32, 35, 36, 38–39, 40, 93
Angelina's (café), 67, 68
anise, 71, 171
Anne of Austria, 68
apple
    doughnut, 8
    tart, 8, 63, 151
    turnover, 8, 63, 142–43
apprentices, 86, 93, 95, 97–98, 103
apricot tart, 8, 55, 148, 150
ascorbic acid, 22
Avice (chef), 74
Aztecs, 68, 69

baba, rum *(babas au rhum)*, 8, 78, 79, 80, 81, 82, 83, *84*, 85, 163, 167–69, 171
baguettes, 8, *17*, 29, 39–40, 60, 91, 92, 106–7, 108–9, 113, 126–27
    history of, 16, 17, 18, 20–22
Bailleux, Louis (writer), 77
Bailly *(pâtisserie)*, 72, 74, 75, 76
bain-marie, 156, 166

baked cherry pancake, 165
baking
    folklore about, 42, 43, 98, 100–1, 121
    history of, 40, 42–45, 47–52, 54–55, 57
barley, 18
bâtards, 8
Baudouin, Victor *(boulanger)*, 30
Baudry, Paul (painter), 80
Bazin *(boulangerie)*, 104, *104*
Béchu *(boulangerie)*, *11*, 13–16, 22, *23*, 24, 31, 32, 36, 38–40, 48
Béchu, Madame, 13, 36
beech wood spades, 10
beets, 69
beignet, 51, 54
belles affaires, 30
Benoist, George-Louis, 90
Benoist, Louis, 90
Benoist, Maximilien-Louis, 88, 89
Benoist, Théophile, 88, 90
Benoist et Fils company, 88, 89, 90
Benoit, Madame (manager), 10, 12, 15, 22, 24, 32, 35, 38
Bertaux, Daniel (sociologist), 93, 95
biologique, 110
biscottes, 14
biscuits, 57
Black Forest cake, 8
blé, 34
Boisguerin, Bernard *(boulanger)*, 95, 96, 97–98, 101–3, 105, 108
bouchées à la reine, 96
Boulangerie Chevreau, *see* Béchu
boules, 32–33

Bourbonneux *(pâtisserie)*, 81
bran, 25–26, 130
bread, 124–25
    baguettes, 8, 16, 17, *17*, 18, 20–22, 29, 39–40, 60, 91, 92, 106–7, 108–9, 113, 126–27
    bâtards, 8
    brioche, 8, 47, 66, 77, 80, 83, 95, 114, 132–34
    country-style, 8, 12, 105–6, 107, 108, 110, 129
    ficelles, 8, 29
    flûte, 8, 22, 108–9, 110
    fougasse, 117, 124, *124*, 131
    French toast, 134
    Kugelhopf, 80, 133–34
    olive and anchovy, 117, 131
    rye, 6, 9, 129
    sourdough, 6, 8, 12, 60, 62, 63, 103, 120, 127–28
    white, 19–20
    whole wheat, 8, 130
    See also pain
brewer's yeast, 9, 18, 19, 21, 42, 45, 47, 55, 60, 62, 63, 69, 83, 95, 105, 109, 125, 126, 129, 130, 132, 135, 139, 168
Brillat-Savarin (writer), 169
    on chocolate, 68–69
brioche, 8, 47, 66, 77, 83, 95, 114, 132–33
    Kugelhopf, 80, 133–34
brotherhoods of bakers, 43
butter cream, 166–67

Caille, Gilles (chef), 153, 154
Canadian Manitoba wheat, 22
canelles, 58
Capetian monks, 42
Carême, Marie-Antonin (chef), 49, 65, 66, 69, 73–76, 81, 158
carolines, 158
Catherine de Medici (wife of Henry II), 52, 55, 59, 66, 73, 158, 166
chambre de pousse, 64
Charlemagne, 91
Charles VII, 170
charlottes, 8, 38
chaussons au pomme, 8, 142–43
chef (raising agent), 62, 129
cherry
    pancake, 165
    tart, 8
chervis, 55
Chevallier, Albert (chef)
    on eighteenth-century gourmands, 72
Chiboust cream, 158
chocolate, 65
    buttercream, 166–67
    éclairs, *159,* 161
    history of, 67–69
    macaroons, 166–67
    puffs, 140–41
choquettes, 160–61
chossons, see turnover
choux bun, 66, 160–61
    See also saint-honores
choux pastry, 65, 66, 73, 158, 160
clafouti, 163, 165
Claude (dairy farmer), 118, 119, *119,* 120, 121
Coltelli, Procopio dei (café proprietor), 66–67
Columbus, Christopher, 69
confréries, 43

cookies
    flaky pastry, 143
    macaroons, 52, 66, 73, 58, 59, 65, 163, 166–67
    See also palmiers
Cortés, Hernan, 69
couches, 109
country-style bread, 8, 12, 105–6, 107, 108, 110
    See also pain de campagne
cream *(crème)*
    almond *(d'amande),* 64, 72, 78, 140, 144, 146–47
    au beurre, 166–67
    butter, 166–67
    Chiboust, 158
    frangipane, 52, 72
    mocha, 76
    pâtissière, 38, 55, 57, 64, 85, 137, 151, 156, 157, 158, 160, 161, 162
    Quillet, 76
croissant, 8, *40,* 47, 48, 63, 83, 88, 95, 96, 97, *136,* 138–41
    origins of, 5, 138
    weighing, 29
croquet, 136
Curnonsky (writer), 153
custard, 148
    raisin custard cake, 165
    tarts, 8, 54, 163, 164, *164,* 165

Dagobert, King, 91
Danièle (dairy farmer), 118, 119, *119,* 120, 121
de Bouffon (writer)
    on wheat, 44
Delessert, Benjamin (industrialist), 69
dépôt de pain, 110, 112
deregulation, 91–92
Dictionary of Cuisine (Dumas), 73–74, 81
Diderot, Denis (encyclopedist), 51

divorce, 67, 158
doughnuts
    cinnamon, 51
    apple, 8
Duchesne *(pâtisserie),* 70, *70*
Dumas, Alexandre (writer), 73, 80, 81, 171
Durand *(pâtissier),* 158, 160
Duthu, François (chef), 80, 82–83, 85, 86, 87

échaudé, 71
éclairs, 8, 66, 68, 158, *159,* 160–61
    chocolate *(au chocolat), 159,* 161
    divorce, 67, 158
    pâte à choux for, 158, 160, 161, 162
    See also carolines; religieuse; saint-honorés; salammbô
Ecole de Boulangerie, 29, 46, *40,* 113–14
Egyptians, 40, 42
einkorn, 44
Elsevier, Daniel, 50
Elsevier, Louis, 50
emmer, 44
Encyclopedie (Diderot), 51
entremets, 49–50, 66
Epiphany cake, 144, *145,* 146–47
espice douce, 51

far, 163, 165
Fauvel, 66, 158
Félix *(pâtisserie),* 76–77, 78
feuillantine, 12
ficelles, 8, 29
fig tart, 55, 150
flaky pastry, 47, 141–42
    apple turnover, 8, 63, 142–43
    chaussons au pomme, 8, 142–43
    cookies, 143
    Epiphany cake, 144, *145,* 146–47
    galette des rois, 64, 135, 144, *145,* 146–47
    palmiers, 8, 63, 143

flaky pastry (continued)
    pâte feuilletée for, 55, 64, 72, 141–42, 143, 144, 146
    sacristains, 135, 143–44
    sticks, 143–44
flans, 8
Flaubert, Gustave, 158
fleur de farine, 19
fleur d'oranger, 71, 72
flûte, 8, 22
flûte Gana, 108–9, 110
Flûte Gana, La *(boulangerie),* 110
folklore about baking, 42, 43, 98, 100–1, 121
fougasse, 117, 124, *124*
    aux olives et anchois, 131
fournil, 4–5
Fournil de Pierre (bakery chain), 107
fours banaux, 120
framboisier, 8, 12, 38
France Gastronomique, La (Curnonsky), 153
Francois, Denis *(boulanger),* 20
frangipane cream, 52, 72
French country bread, 129
    See also pain de campagne
French-style sourdough, 127–28
    See also pain au levain
French toast, 134
friands, 51

galette, 115
    rye-flour, 19
galette des rois, 64, 135, 144, *145,* 146–47
Ganachaud *(boulanger),* 108–9, 110
Ganachaud *(boulangerie),* 145, *145*
gâteau basque, 149, *149*
gâteaux
    See individual cake and pastry names
gâteaux des rois, 72
    See also galette des rois

Gauls, 40, 42, 50
génoises, 73, 76
gimblettes, 71
Giono, Jean (writer), 33, 117
Gogh, Vincent Willem van, 16
Gonesse, 19–20, 21
gorenflot, 81
Gouffé, Jules *(pâtissier),* 77
grand panetier, 42
Grands Moulins de Paris, 46, 103, 107, 125
Greeks, 42, 117
Grottshalk, Alfred (writer), 138
Guyot (master baker), 3 5, 6, 8 10, 16, 32

hachis Parmentier, 44
Harvard, Jacques (agricultural engineer), 114
Henry II, 55, 66
Henry III, 81
honey, 54
Honoré, Saint, 43, 159

James, Saint, 171
jesuit, 63–64, 135
Jeudon, Jean *(boulanger),* 109, 110, 112, 145, *145*
Joan of Arc, 112
Julien frères *(pâtissiers),* 81, 82, 169
jute cloth, 3–4, 7, 109

Kamir, Basil (entrepreneur), 108
Kugelhopf, 80, 133–34

laboratoire, 5
Lacaille *(boulangerie),* 116, *116*
Lacam, Pierre *(pâtissier)* 71, 72, 77, 82
Ladurée *(pâtissier),* 58
La femme du boulanger (film), 33–34
Laguepière (chef), 74
Larousse Gastronomique (Grottshalk), 138

La Varenne (writer), 50–51, 52, 54, 55, 57, 151
Lazarus, Saint, 42, 102
leaven, 40, 60, 62–63, 106, 109
    See also brewer's yeast
Lefevre, *see* Uncle Farine
lemon tart, 8, 58, 152–53
Lenôtre, Gaston *(pâtissier),* 64, 87
levain, 8, 60
    See also leaven
Le Ventre de Paris (Zola), 148
levure artificiel
    See brewer's yeast
Lion (baker), 132
Livre de la Pâtisserie (Gouffe), 77
Louis, Saint, 51, 120
Louis XIII, 68
Louis XIV, 43, 55
Louis XV, 80
Louis XVI, 20, 47, 138

macarons au chocolat, 166–67
macaroons, 52, 66, 73, 163
    chocolate, 166–67
    pistachio, 58, 59, 65
madeleines, 50, 58, 59, 73, 76, 163, 171–72
maisons
    defined, 48
marchands de vins, 21
Maria-Theresa of Hungary, 52
Marie-Antoinette, 20, 47, 138
Mémorial de la Pâtisserie (Lacam), 77
mère (raising agent), 129
meringue, 65, 73, 74, 75, 77, 158, 163, 167
Merle (critic)
    on the Revolutionary years, 72
millefeuille, 12
millers, 18, 34–35
mills, 18–19, 34–35, 45, 60, 107, 108, 114, 120

mitron, 4–5

Mitterand, President Francois, 91

mocha cream, 76

Montezuma, 69

Morand (pastry chef), 5, 9

Moreau, Claude *(patissier),* 83, *84,* 85

Moulin Brulé, 18

Moulin de la Gallette (painting), 19

Moulin de la Vierge, Le *(boulangerie),* 37, *37,* 41, 108, 124, *124*

Moulin Rouge, 19

Musée du Pain, 21

Napoleon Bonaparte, 69, 74, 75

Napoleon III, 6

nattes, 12

navettes, 12

Niarkos (Greek general), 52

olive and anchovy bread, 117, 131
    See also fougasse

opéra cake, 8, 38, 68

orange blossom water, 71, 76, 134, 172

oublies, 82

ovens, parish, 120

Pagnol, Marcel (filmmaker), 33

pain, 8, 32

pain au lait, 47, 135, 137

pain au levain, 6, 106, 120, 127–28
    See also sourdough bread

pain au raisin, 8, 47, 48, 137

pain aux céréales, 8, 114

pain brié, 115

pain chocolat, 8, 41, 47, 48, 63, *130,* 140–41

pain complet, 8
    See also whole wheat bread

pain d'antan, 120

pain d'autrefois, 103, 105

pain de campagne, 6, 7, 8, 32, 106, 109, 114, 124, *124,* 129
    See also country-style bread

pain de courge, 115

pain de fabrication française
    defined, 107

pain de maison
    defined, 107

pain de Mme. de Montpensier, 13

pain de Paris, 126

pain d'épice, 115, 170–71

pain de seigle, 6

pain de son, 130

pain mollet, 108

pain perdu, 134

pain poilâne, 106

Painwich, 108

palmiers, 8, 63, 143

pancake, baked cherry, 165

Pantagruel (Rabelais), 54

Parfait boulanger (Parmentier), 43, 44

Paris-Brest, 158, 160

parish ovens, 120

Paris mange son pain (film), 102

Parmentier (agronomist), 40, 43–45

pasté au poyres
    See tarte au poire

pastés, 52, 55
    defined, 51

Pasteur, Louis (microbiologist), 57

pasties, 51

pastillas, 51

Pastissier Francois (La Varenne), 50–51, 52, 57

pastry cream, 157

pâte à choux, 158, 160, 161, 162
    See also choux pastry

pâte brisée, 148–49, 151, 152, 155

pâte feuilletée, 55, 64, 72, 141–42, 143, 144, 146

pâte sablée, 155–56

pâtisserie
    almond tarts *(amandines),* 8, 163
    baba, rum *(babas au rhum),* 8, 78, 79, 80, 81, 82, 83, *84,* 85, 163, 167–69, 171
    baked cherry pancake, 165
    charlottes, 8, 38
    clafouti, 163, *164,* 165
    éclairs, 8, 66, 67, 68, 158, *159,* 160–62
    far, 165
    framboisier, 8, 12, 38
    history of, 47–52, 54–55, 57, 66–69, 71–78
    macaroons, 52, 58, 59, 65, 66, 73, 163, 166–67
    madeleines, 50, 58, 59, 73, 76, 163, 171–72
    meringues, 65, 73, 74, 75, 77, 158, 163, 167
    operas, 8, 38, 68
    pain d'épice, 115, 170–71
    pastry cream for, 55, 57, 64, 85, 157, 158
    raisin custard cake, 165
    savarin, 8, 81, 169–70
    spice cake, 115, 170–71

Pâtissier Moderne (Bailleux), 77

Pâtissier Pittoresque (Careme), 75

Pâtissier Royal, Le (Careme), 73, 76, 158

Paumier, Madeleine, 171

peach tart, 55

pear tart, 8, 55, 151

Peltier *(pâtisserie),* 83

pensée, 81

petit fours, 66, 74, 78, 96, 160

petit pains, 73

pétrins, 21

Phoenicians, 40

Physiology of Taste, The (Brillat-Savarin), 68, 169

Picasso, Pablo, 131

pièces-montées, 74–75

Pierre, François, *see* La Varenne

Pimpinella anisum, 71

pine nut tart, 149, *149*, 151–52
plancheoirs, 42
plonge, 5, 97
plum tart, 55
Poilâne, Lionel *(boulanger),* 105–6, 108, 109, 120
point de cuisson, 92
Poujauran, Jean-Luc *(boulanger),* 56, *56,* 58–60, 62, 63–65, 108, 149, 151
Poujauran *(boulangerie), 53, 56,* 57–59, 61, *61*
preservatives, 92
Prevert, Jacques (narrator), 102
Prevert, Pierre (filmmaker), 102
Procope's (café), 67
Proust, Marcel (writer), 50, 172
puits d'amour, 85

Quillet *(pâtisserie),* 76

Rabelais, François (writer), 54
raisin custard cake, 165
raising agents
   See brewer's yeast; leaven
religieuse, 158
Remembrance of Things Past (Proust), 172
Renoir, Pierre-Auguste (painter), 19
richelieu, 81
Risleff, Countess, 80
Rollet *(pâtisserie),* 77–78
Romans, 42, 50, 55, 117, 141
rosewater, 55, 71
rouleurs, 35–36
royale, 12
rum baba, 8, 78, 79, 80, 81, 82, 83, *84,* 85, 163, 167–69, 171
rye, 18, 19, 171
   bread, 6, 9, 129

sablées, 149, *149*
sable pastry, 155–56
Saccharomyces cerevisiae, 62
   See also brewer's yeast
sacristains, 135, 143–44
saint-honorés, 66, 72, 158
   See also choux bun
salammbô, 158, 162
Santiago de Compostela, 171
savarin, 8, 81, 169–70
shortcrust pastry, 148–49
Sorel, Agnes (Charles VII's mistress), 170
sourdough bread, 6, 8, 12, 60, 62, 63, 103, 120, 127–28
spades, beech wood, 10
spice cake, 115, 170–71
spices, 51–52, 170
sponge cake
   See madeleines
Springer, Baron (industrialist), 21, 47
Stanislas I, King of Poland, 80, 167, 171
Stohrer *(pâtissier),* 78, 79, 80, 167
Stohrer *(pâtisserie),* 78, 79, *79,* 81, 82–83, 84, *84,* 85–86, 87, 169
Stone Oven, The (bakery chain), 92, 107
strawberry tart, 55, 156
sugar, 52, 54, 68, 69
sur poulish, 109

talemeliers, 42
Talleyrand, 74
tallying sticks, 34, 42
tartelettes, 8, 163
tartes
   au citron, 152–53
   au poire, 151
   aux abricots, 150
   aux fraises, 156
   aux pignons, 57–58, 151–52

Tatin, 153, *154,* 155
   See also tarts
tartines, 6
tarts, 54–55, 73
   almond *(amandines),* 8, 163
   apple, 8, 63, 151
   apricot, 8, 55, 148, 150
   cherry, 8, 148
   crème pâtissiere for, 38, 55, 57, 64, 85, 137, 151, 156, 157, 158, 160, 161, 162
   custard, 8, 54, 163, 164, *164,* 165
   fromage blanc, 54
   fig, 55, 150
   lemon, 8, 58, 152–53
   pastry cream for, 38, 55, 57, 64, 85, 137, 151, 156, 157, 158, 160, 161, 162
   pâte brisée for, 148–49, 151, 152, 155
   pâte sablée for, 155–56
   peach, 55
   pear, 8, 55, 148, 151
   pine nut, 57–58, 149, *149,* 151–52
   plum, 55
   sable pastry for, 155–56
   shortcrust pastry for, 148, 150
   strawberry, 55, 156
   See also tartes
Tatin, Caroline, 153
Tatin, Stephanie, 153
terroir, 114
Thousand and One Nights, 167
tordu, 109–10
tougnole, 110
tour, 5, 138
tourte, 54
   defined, 51
   de racines, 55
Train Bleu (restaurant), 108
Triticum vulgare, 44
trois-frères, 81

turnover, 54
    apple, 8, 63, 142–43

Uncle Farine, 35, 36, 103
upside-down loaves, 10

vainilla (vanilla), 69, 71
Vatel *(maître d'hôtel),* 73
Viennese buns, 135, 137
    raisin, 137

viennoiserie, 29, 47, 88
    chocolate puffs, 140–41
    croissants, 5, 8, 29, *40,* 47, 48, 63, 83, 88, 95,
        96, 97, *130,* 138–41
    pain au lait, 47, 135, 137
    pain au raisin, 8, 47, 48, 137
    pain chocolat, 8, 41, 47, 48, 63, *136,* 140–41
    Viennese buns, 135, 137
vitamin C, 22
vol-au-vent, 85

wheat, 16, 18–20
    Canadian Manitoba, 22
    French 22
    history of, 44–45

wheelers, 35–36
white bread, 19–20
    See also baguettes
whole wheat bread, 8
    with bran, 130
windmills, 18–19, 60

yeast, brewer's, 9, 18, 19, 21, 42, 45, 47, 55, 60,
    62, 63, 69, 83, 105, 109, 125, 126, 129,
    130, 132, 135, 139, 168

Zang (Prussian officer), 21, 47, 135
Zola, Emile, 148

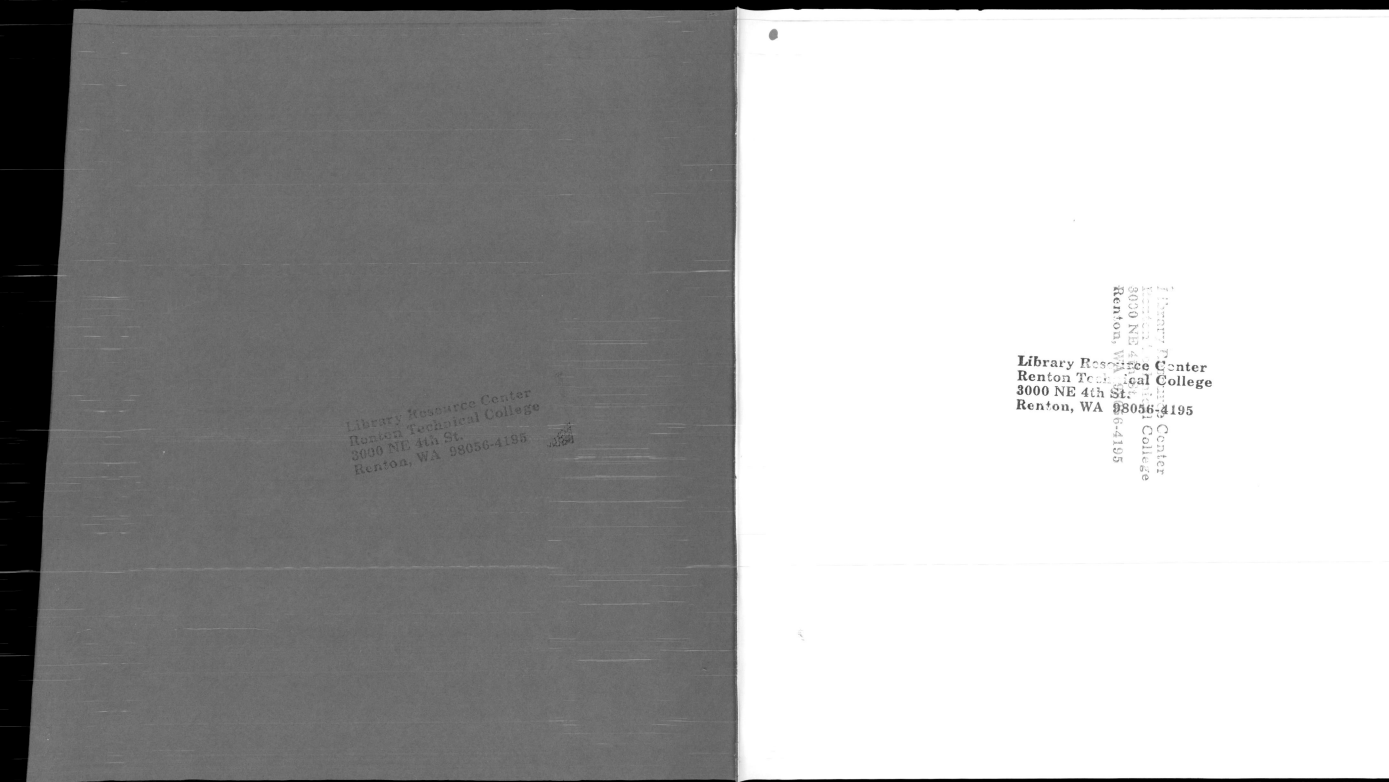